MAY

A MONTH OF IDEAS AT YOUR FINGERTIPS!

GRADES 4–6

WRITTEN BY

Chris Christensen, Carol Felts, Dr. Linda Flynn, Beth Gress,
Peggy W. Hambright, Simone Lepine, Elizabeth H. Lindsay, Thad H. McLaurin,
Barbara Samuels, Mary Lou Schlosser, Marsha Schmus, Judith Shutter,
Mary Spaulding, Elizabeth Tanzi, Patricia Twohey, Stephanie Willett-Smith

EDITED BY

Lynn Bemer Coble, Thad H. McLaurin, Carol Rawleigh,
Jennifer Rudisill, Gina Sutphin, Christine A. Thuman

ILLUSTRATED BY

Jennifer T. Bennett, Pam Crane,
Teresa Davidson, Clevell Harris,
Sheila Krill, Rob Mayworth,
Rebecca Saunders, Barry Slate

TYPESET BY

Lynette Maxwell

COVER DESIGNED BY

Jennifer T. Bennett

www.themailbox.com

©1996 by THE EDUCATION CENTER, INC.
All rights reserved.
ISBN# 1-56234-155-3

Manufactured in the United States
10 9 8 7 6 5 4 3

TABLE OF CONTENTS

May Calendar

National Physical Fitness And Sports Month

Promoting fitness and physical well-being is the focus of National Physical Fitness And Sports Month. Help in this effort by encouraging your students to participate in physical activities. Have students keep a log of the physical activities they participate in during the month of May. Discuss how establishing a healthy exercise routine can improve a person's physical condition and overall well-being.

Older Americans Month

May is Older Americans Month. Recognize the accomplishments of older Americans by hosting a luncheon in honor of local elderly people. Allow each student to invite one older person who is important to him. Before the luncheon, use construction paper and an overhead projector to make a silhouette of each student. Have each student sign his silhouette with a note of thanks before presenting it to his special guest during the luncheon. Both your students and their guests will grow closer from this shared experience.

Asian Pacific Heritage Month

Asian Pacific Heritage Month provides us with the chance to recognize and celebrate the accomplishments of Asian Pacific Americans. Have students work in pairs to research a noted Asian Pacific American. Then ask the pairs to share their findings with their peers. Create a bulletin board featuring these notable citizens and their achievements.

National Bike Month

In an effort to recognize the widespread use of bicycles for transportation and recreation, special events are held across the country during National Bike Month. Get your students into the biking spirit by having each one design a bicycle safety poster reminding bikers of proper maintenance and operating procedures. Display these posters around your school.

National Photo Month

National Photo Month is observed during May to increase public interest in the art of photography. Promote photography among your students by creating a "Photo Wall." Encourage each student to bring in a photograph he has taken. Have each child write a few descriptive sentences about his photo. Display this information with the photo on a bulletin board titled "Captured Moments."

(Turn the page for more…)

3

15—Peace Officer Memorial Day

Peace Officer Memorial Day honors police officers who have given their lives in the line of duty. Discuss the important role police and other peace officers play in our society. Ask students what the world might be like without the efforts of these individuals. Have students make individual cards of thanks for members of your local police force.

20—Anniversary Of Amelia Earhart's Transatlantic Flight

On this day in 1932, Amelia Earhart became the first woman to fly solo across the Atlantic Ocean. She flew from Harbor Grace, Newfoundland, to Londonderry, Ireland, in less than 14 hours and became a pioneer in the women's aviation movement. Discuss the importance of being a pioneer in a field. Have students cite examples of other pioneers whose achievements or discoveries have had an effect on our world.

1—May Day

People recognize May Day as a time to celebrate the new life brought forth by spring. Have your students brainstorm a list of the signs of spring that have appeared in recent weeks. Record these on a poster titled "The Signs Of Spring." Take your students on a walk around the school to search for additional signs of spring to add to the list.

12—Limerick Day

Limerick Day honors Edward Lear, a noted limerick writer and author of *Book Of Nonsense,* who was born on this day in 1812. In honor of this occasion, have each student compose an original limerick. Invite your students to share their limericks orally, and then display the written poems around your classroom.

25—Anniversary Of The Constitutional Convention

The first Constitutional Convention convened in Philadelphia, Pennsylvania, on this day in 1787. Delegates from seven states attended the opening of the convention. Review the rights outlined in the U. S. Constitution with your students. List reasons why it is important to have such a document outlining individual rights. Challenge students to draft a new amendment that they would like to see added to the Constitution.

Teacher's May Resource Calendar
A Handy List Of Special Days

May was most likely named in honor of the Roman goddess Maia, the mother of Hermes. Anglo-Saxons referred to the month as *Tri-Milchi* because their cows were supposed to give milk three times a day during this month as a result of having fed on the new, spring grass.

5 Nelly Bly, women's rights advocate and American journalist, was born on this day in 1867.

6 Robert Peary, discoverer of the North Pole, was born in Cresson, Pennsylvania, on this day in 1856.

7 The British passenger liner *Lusitania*—suspected by the Germans of carrying ammunition for the British during World War I—sank off the coast of Ireland after being torpedoed by a German submarine on this day in 1915.

9 John Brown, abolitionist and leader of an attack on Harpers Ferry, was born on this day in 1800.

10 On this day in 1994, Nelson Mandela was inaugurated as president of South Africa.

12 Florence Nightingale, champion of the nursing profession, was born in Florence, Italy, on this day in 1820.

13 World heavyweight boxing champion, Joe Louis, was born on this day in 1914.

14 Gabriel Daniel Fahrenheit—German physicist who introduced the use of mercury in thermometers—was born in Danzig, Germany, on this day in 1686.

17 On this day in 1954, the Supreme Court ruled unanimously that the existence of separate educational facilities based on race was not constitutional.

19 Malcolm X, civil rights activist, was born in Omaha, Nebraska, on this day in 1925.

22 National Maritime Day is observed on this day.

24 In 1883 the Brooklyn Bridge—connecting Manhattan and Brooklyn—opened as the longest suspension bridge in the world, spanning a distance of 1,595 feet.

29 John Fitzgerald Kennedy, the 35th president of the United States, was born in Brookline, Massachusetts, on this day in 1917.

31 American poet Walt Whitman was born on this day in 1819.

May Clip Art

Use on the following items:

- letters to parents
- games
- nametags

- notes to students
- homework assignments
- newsletters

- awards
- learning centers
- bulletin boards

CLASSROOM TIMES

Teacher: _____   Date: _____

Highlights

Don't Forget!

Hats Off To...

Special Events

Help Wanted

FREE-TIME FUN for May!

Tackle these 20 terrific tasks when you finish your work.

Monday	Tuesday	Wednesday	Thursday	Friday
Cartoon Art Appreciation Week is May 1–5. Design your own cartoon character in honor of this week. 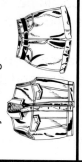	Make a list of all the words you can think of that end with the suffix -able. ### -able	Write a letter to a friend or relative who lives in another city or state.	Make a list of ten memorable events from this school year. 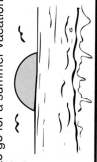 Field Trip!	List ten things you can re-cycle. 
May is National Egg Month. List five uses for eggs.	Make a Mother's Day card for your mother or for another important woman in your life. Happy Mother's Day	List ten ways to use a cup.	In honor of National Straw-berry Month, write a recipe that contains strawberries as an ingredient. 	Design a uniform for stu-dents in your school. Illus-trate your design. 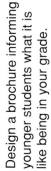
Estimate the length of your desk in inches. Then use a ruler to test your estimation.	What is the difference be-tween an *annual* flower and a *perennial* flower?	Use the words *who's* and *whose* in the same sentence. ### who's ### whose	How many months have 31 days?	List five places you would like to go for a summer vacation.
What is your favorite physical activity? List five *other* fun ways to get exercise.	National Cat Lovers Week is in May. Make a list of famous felines.	May is National Hamburger Month. Make a list of all the toppings you like to eat on a hamburger. Then draw the burger. 	Design a brochure informing younger students what it is like being in your grade. 5th	Write a note of appreciation to your teacher. Thank You

Note To The Teacher: Have each student staple a copy of this page inside a file folder. Direct students to store their completed work inside their folders.

Desktag: Duplicate student copies onto construction paper. Have each student personalize and decorate his pattern; then laminate the patterns and use them as desktags during the month of May.

Award: Duplicate multiple copies. Keep them handy at your desk during the month of May. When a student earns an award, write his name, the subject, and the date on the appropriate lines.

Simply "Purr–r–r–fect"!!

_____

has had a super week.
Keep up the good work!

_____
(Teacher)

_____
(Date)

We're Having A Carnival!

A Year-End Celebration Of Books

Looking for a motivating way to end the school year? Or would you simply like to try some fun, literature-related games to liven up those last days before the summer break? Whatever your purpose, this reading carnival will encourage your students to carry those hard-earned reading habits into the summer!

by Simone Lepine

A Reading Carnival

Use the following directions to transform your room into a carnival to celebrate reading. Plan for half the class to run the carnival booths while the other half plays the games; then switch. Or host the carnival for another class on your grade level. If you're not up to organizing a carnival, never fear! Simply use the games on pages 12–16 as centers in your classroom!

Getting Ready

1. Three weeks before Day One, form cooperative groups by having each student sign up for one of the following categories: biography, humor, realistic fiction, poetry, science fiction, historical fiction, folklore, books in a series, books made into movies, or how-to books. Limit each group to two or three members to ensure that each category gets represented at the carnival.
2. Instruct each group to read a total of six different books from its category, with each group member reading a different book. (See pages 19 and 87 for suggested titles.)
3. Solicit for donations of bookmarks to give away on carnival day.
4. Follow the directions for Days One through Five to prepare for and conduct the carnival.

Day One: Make Mini-Review Booklets

Each person who participates in a carnival game will receive a mini-review booklet about one of the novels represented at that booth. To make a supply of these booklets, duplicate six copies of the form on page 17 for each group. Have each group member complete one form for each book he read. Then duplicate copies of the completed forms. (To determine the total number of copies needed of each booklet, divide the number of students in the class [or the invited class] by *six*—the number of books read by each group). Give each group its copies along with instructions to cut off the margins and fold the pages into booklets as shown.

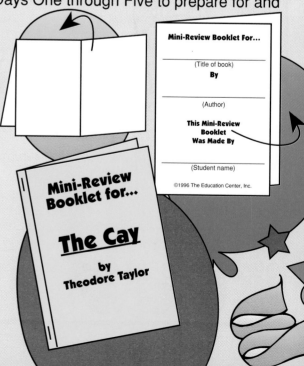

Mini-Review Booklet For...

(Title of book)
By

(Author)

This Mini-Review Booklet Was Made By

(Student name)

©1996 The Education Center, Inc.

Mini-Review Booklet for...

The Cay

by Theodore Taylor

Days Two, Three, And Four: Make The Games And Set Up Booths

Duplicate the appropriate game card for each group from pages 12–16. Direct the group to follow the directions to make six copies of its carnival game. Provide groups with space to set up their booths. Next direct each group to decide who will be the mini-review booklet distributor and the game director.

Day Five: Enjoy The Carnival

Have each group man its carnival booth. When the participants arrive, divide them into ten groups; then assign each group a starting booth. Use a designated signal to let groups know when it's time to switch to the next booth. Each time a participant completes a game, have the mini-review booklet distributor allow the player to choose a review booklet that interests him. At the end of the carnival, present each participant with a bookmark.

Pam Crane

Book-Boosting Balloons

Encourage your students to clown around with a variety of books. Duplicate, enlarge, and color the clown from page 18. Next cut out ten large, colorful balloons. On each balloon write one of the literature categories used for the carnival. Staple the balloon cutouts to the board in an attractive arrangement; then connect them to the clown's hand with lengths of black yarn. Enlist a student to write in the names and authors of the books that belong to each category. Encourage students to add additional titles to each category. When students are looking for good books to read, point them to the board for some student-tested suggestions.

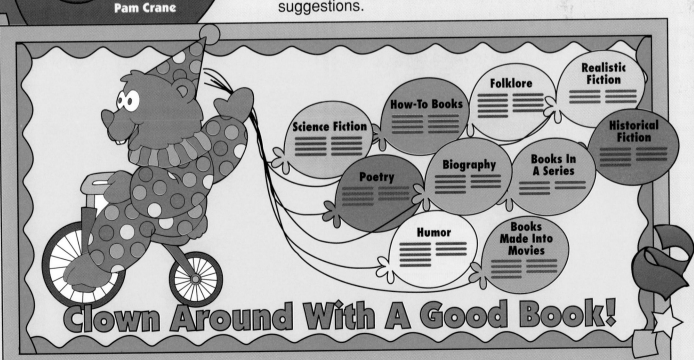

Clown Around With A Good Book!

Game 1—Drop Into The Future

Book Category: Science Fiction

Materials: six shirt boxes, colored markers, scissors, masking tape, six marbles, six small paper cups

How To Make The Game:

1. Turn the top lid of each shirt box upside down. Mark and cut out ten marble-sized holes on the inside of each top lid. Designate one hole as the winning hole by circling it in red.
2. Decorate each top lid so that it advertises one of the books read by the group. Write each book's title and author, along with several adjectives that describe the book, in the spaces between the holes.
3. Cut five slits in the lip of each paper cup to create folding tabs as shown.
4. Attach each cup underneath a winning hole by taping the tabs to the lid.
5. Cut another marble-sized hole in a corner of the lower lid to make an exit hole for any marbles that fall through the nonwinning holes.
6. Tape each upside-down top lid to its matching lower lid as shown. The sides of the top lid form walls to keep the marble from rolling away.

How To Play The Game: Have the player choose a box and place a marble on its playing surface. Then direct him to tilt the box as he tries to get the marble into the winning hole. If he gets the marble in the winning hole, turn the box over to retrieve the marble from the cup. If his marble goes into the wrong hole, tilt the box until the marble exits at the bottom corner. Give each player three tries.

Game 2—Find The Fake Fact

Book Category: Biography

Materials: 30 unlined index cards, fine-tipped colored markers, six rubber bands

How To Make The Game: Make a set of five cards for each book that was read by your group members. On four of the cards, write a sentence stating a true fact about the story on the front of the card and the word "Fact" on the back. On the fifth card, write a fake fact sentence on the front and the word "Fake" on the back. Place a rubber band around each set of five cards.

How To Play The Game: Instruct the player to choose a set of cards. Shuffle the cards and place them sentence-side up in a row in front of the player. Have the player read each card and point to the fake fact card. Beginning with the first card, turn over the cards one at a time to see if the player is a winner. Let each player try three different card sets.

Game 3—Putt In A Cup

Book Category: How-To Books

Materials: three golf balls, a putter, three poster-size pieces of stiff cardboard, scissors, a black marker, six large paper cups, six right-angle triangles cut from cardboard, masking tape

How To Make The Game: Divide each piece of cardboard into two halves by drawing a vertical black line. Use a paper cup to trace a circular opening at the bottom of each half as shown; then cut out each circular space. Decorate the front panels above each hole with the title and author of a different how-to book. Use masking tape to attach a cup to the back of the cardboard behind each hole (see figure 2). Attach two cardboard triangles to the back of each sheet to support it. Line up the gameboards side by side. Place a strip of masking tape about six to eight feet away from each poster.

How To Play The Game: Give the player the putter and a ball and instruct her to stand behind the masking-tape mark. Have the player putt the golf ball through a hole and into a cup to win.

fig. 1

fig. 2

Game 4—Coming To A Theater Near You

Book Category: Books That Have Become Movies

Materials: six sheets of poster board, scissors, 60 inches of self-adhesive Velcro®, six Ping-Pong® balls, masking tape, colored markers

How To Make The Game: Press two lengths of loop-sided Velcro® around the middle of each ball to form perpendicular, intersecting lines. Draw a six-inch circle in the center of each poster-board sheet. Divide the hook-sided Velcro® into six equal lengths. Cut apart each Velcro® length and press the pieces around the inside of the circle. Write the title of a book and its author on each poster along with comments that tell why reading the book is better than seeing the movie. Thumbtack the posters to a bulletin board or tape them to a wall. On the floor, place a strip of tape eight to ten feet away from each poster.

How To Play The Game: Have each player choose a poster and line up behind the masking-tape line with his Ping-Pong® ball. Give the player three chances to throw the ball and get it to stick to the poster's circle.

Game 5—Wheel Of Historical Fiction

Book Category: Historical Fiction

Materials: a 14-inch cardboard circle (cut from a cardboard box or donated from a pizza restaurant), a 2" x 6" strip of heavy black paper, a ruler, colored markers, one brad fastener, two clothespins, scissors

How To Make The Game: Use the ruler and a marker to divide the cardboard circle into six equal sections as shown. Write the name of a different book in each section. Cut a large cardboard arrow from the black paper. Connect the arrow to the center of the circle with the paper brad so that the arrow spins easily.

How To Play The Game: Have each player choose two books by clipping a clothespin to each of those sections. Allow the player two spins to get the arrow to stop on a section he chose and win.

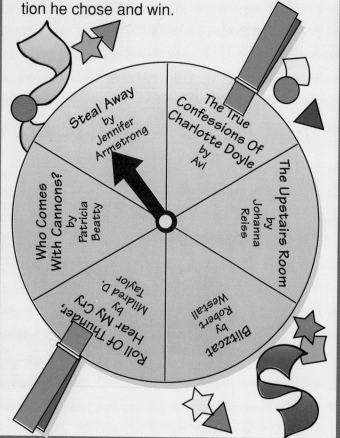

Game 6—Book Bopping

Book Category: Humor

Materials: six clean, half-gallon milk cartons; bulletin-board paper; scissors; clear tape; colored markers; fine-tipped markers; six zippered plastic bags, each filled with one cup of flour; two chairs; a six-foot-long wooden board; masking tape; three beanbags

How To Make The Game: Place a bag of flour inside each milk carton to weigh it down. Close and tape the top opening. Cover each milk carton with bulletin-board paper, using clear tape to hold the paper in place. On each carton's front, write the title and author of a different book. Decorate at least one side of each carton with an illustration or a written description of a funny scene from the book. Place the backs of the chairs about five feet apart; then balance the wooden board on the backs of the chairs. Arrange the milk cartons in a row on the board as shown. Place a strip of tape on the floor eight to ten feet away from the board. Place the beanbags on the tape.

How To Play The Game: Have each player stand behind the line and throw the beanbags one at a time. Give each player three tries to knock at least one milk carton off the board and win.

Game 7—Ping-Pong® Game

Book Category: Books In A Series

Materials: six medium-sized boxes, three Ping-Pong® balls, bulletin-board paper, scissors, clear tape, colored markers, masking tape, a ruler

How To Make The Game: Cover each of the boxes with bulletin-board paper, using clear tape to hold the paper in place. On the front of each box, write the name of the series and three to five book titles that represent it. Line up the boxes against a wall in a straight line, spacing them an equal distance apart. Mark a distance six feet away with a strip of masking tape; then place the Ping-Pong® balls on the tape.

How To Play The Game: Have a player stand behind the marked line and bounce the Ping-Pong® balls one at a time toward the boxes. If he lands at least one of the balls in a box, he wins.

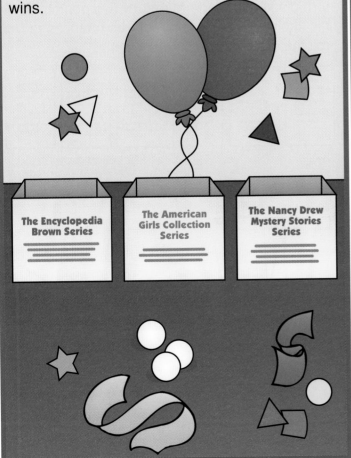

Game 8—Hide 'N' Seek Poetry

Book Category: Poetry

Materials: six shoeboxes without lids, bulletin-board paper, clear tape, colored markers, fine-tipped markers, two tennis balls

How To Make The Game: Cover each shoebox with bulletin-board paper, using tape to hold the paper in place. Turn each box bottom-side up. Write a title and author of a different book on the end of each box. Decorate the sides and bottom of each box with samples of poetry from the book it promotes. Line up the boxes in two groups of three.

How To Play The Game: Have two players stand with their backs to the boxes. Hide a tennis ball under one of the boxes in each set. Ask the players to turn around. Then have each player call out the poet's name from the box he thinks is hiding a tennis ball. Give each player two tries to win.

Game 9—Book-Character Ring Toss

Book Category: Realistic Fiction

Materials: six playground cones, construction paper of different colors, scissors, glue, clear tape, a black marker, three paper plates, a ruler, masking tape

How To Make The Game: Choose a favorite character from each of the six fiction books read by your group. Create a likeness of each character from construction paper. Write each character's name on the corresponding figure with a black marker; then tape each figure to a different playground cone. Arrange the cones in a triangular pattern. Next make rings by cutting the centers from paper plates—without going through the outside edges. Lay a strip of masking tape on the floor six feet away from the cones.

How To Play The Game: Have the player stand behind the marked line, and toss the three rings one at a time. If he rings one of the characters, he wins.

Salamanca Tree Hiddle

Game 10—Book-Bet Board

Book Category: Folklore

Materials: six sheets of white poster board, colored markers, a die pattern from page 17 duplicated on light-colored construction paper, scissors, clear tape, two game markers (coins or plastic game pieces)

How To Make The Game: Write the title and author of each book read by group members on a different poster. Decorate the posters to advertise the books; then line up the posters side by side on the floor.

To make the die, cut out the die pattern. Write the titles and authors of the six books read by group members on the die's blank faces, one title and author on each face. Fold the tabs and faces along the lines, securing them with clear tape.

How To Play The Game: Have each player in turn place two markers on any two posters of his choice. Give the player three chances to roll the die and get a match to win.

BIG MEN BIG COUNTRY
A Collection Of American Tall Tales
by Paul R. Walker

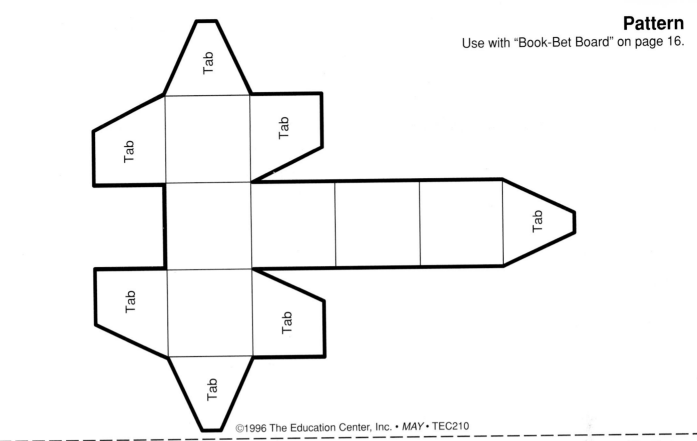

Tab

Tab

Tab

Tab

Tab

Tab

Tab

©1996 The Education Center, Inc. • *MAY* • TEC210

What This Book Is About:

Mini-Review Booklet For...

(Title of book)

By

(Author)

This Mini-Review Booklet Was Made By

(Student name)

©1996 The Education Center, Inc.

The Best Part Of This Book:

Why You Will Like This Book:

Pattern

Use with "Book-Boosting Balloons" on page 11.

Toss Around These Terrific Tomes!

Biography
Boy: Tales Of Childhood by Roald Dahl
Calamity Jane: Her Life And Her Legend by Doris Faber
Colin Powell: A Biography by Jim Haskins
Helen Keller's Teacher by Margaret Davidson
Homesick: My Own Story by Jean Fritz
Lost Star: The Story Of Amelia Earhart by Patricia Lauber

Books Made Into Movies
The Incredible Journey by Sheila Burnford
The Indian In The Cupboard by Lynne R. Banks
Jumanji by Chris Van Allsburg
Mrs. Frisby & The Rats Of NIMH by Robert C. O'Brien
Sounder by William H. Armstrong
The Witches by Roald Dahl

Folklore
American Tall Tales by Mary P. Osborne
Big Men, Big Country: A Collection Of American Tall Tales by Paul R. Walker
Cut From The Same Cloth: American Women Of Myth, Legend, And Tall Tale by Robert San Souci
John Henry And His Mighty Hammer by Patricia A. Jensen
Mike Fink by Steven Kellogg
Sally Ann Thunder Ann Whirlwind Crockett: A Tall Tale by Steven Kellogg

Poetry
Dream Keeper: And Other Poems by Langston Hughes
Falling Up by Shel Silverstein
Poems Of Childhood by Eugene Field
Something Big Has Been Here by Jack Prelutsky
Talking Like The Rain: A First Book Of Poems by X. J. Kennedy
Where The Sidewalk Ends: Poems And Drawings by Shel Silverstein

How-To Books
How To Bead Earrings: An Artistic Approach by Lori S. Berry
How To Be An Inventor by Murray Suid
How To Become A Star Athlete by Tim Conroy
How To Draw Cartoons by Susannah Bradley
Running by Jeff Savage
Soccer Techniques In Pictures by Michael Brown

Science Fiction
Aliens For Breakfast by Jonathan Etra and Stephanie Spinner
Aliens In The Family by Margaret Mahy
Journey To The Center Of The Earth by Jules Verne
My Teacher Flunked The Planet by Bruce Coville
My Teacher Glows In The Dark by Bruce Coville
Twenty Thousand Leagues Under The Sea by Jules Verne

Book In A Series
The American Girls Collection series by various authors
The Boxcar Children Mysteries series by Gertrude C. Warner
The Culpepper Adventures series by Gary Paulsen
The Encyclopedia Brown series by Donald J. Sobol
The Hardy Boys series by Franklin W. Dixon
The Nancy Drew Mystery Stories series by Carolyn Keene

Note To The Teacher: Use this list and the list on page 87 with "Getting Ready" on page 10. Books on Historical Fiction, Realistic Fiction, and Humor are listed on page 87.

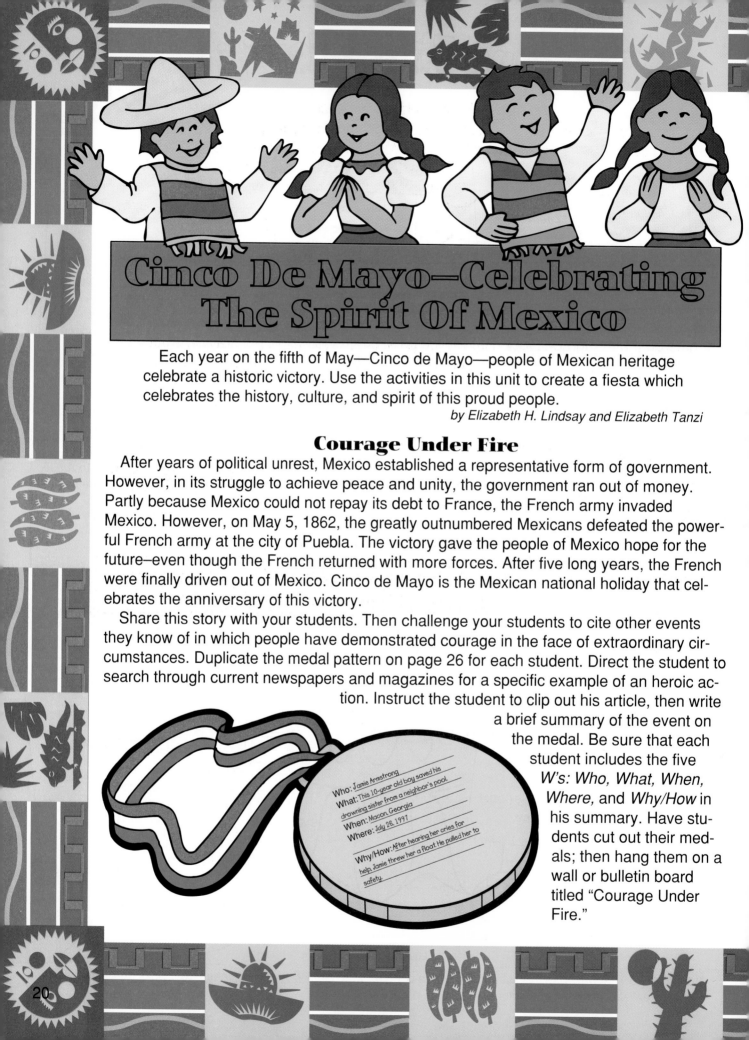

Cinco De Mayo—Celebrating The Spirit Of Mexico

Each year on the fifth of May—Cinco de Mayo—people of Mexican heritage celebrate a historic victory. Use the activities in this unit to create a fiesta which celebrates the history, culture, and spirit of this proud people.

by Elizabeth H. Lindsay and Elizabeth Tanzi

Courage Under Fire

After years of political unrest, Mexico established a representative form of government. However, in its struggle to achieve peace and unity, the government ran out of money. Partly because Mexico could not repay its debt to France, the French army invaded Mexico. However, on May 5, 1862, the greatly outnumbered Mexicans defeated the powerful French army at the city of Puebla. The victory gave the people of Mexico hope for the future–even though the French returned with more forces. After five long years, the French were finally driven out of Mexico. Cinco de Mayo is the Mexican national holiday that celebrates the anniversary of this victory.

Share this story with your students. Then challenge your students to cite other events they know of in which people have demonstrated courage in the face of extraordinary circumstances. Duplicate the medal pattern on page 26 for each student. Direct the student to search through current newspapers and magazines for a specific example of an heroic action. Instruct the student to clip out his article, then write a brief summary of the event on the medal. Be sure that each student includes the five *W's: Who, What, When, Where,* and *Why/How* in his summary. Have students cut out their medals; then hang them on a wall or bulletin board titled "Courage Under Fire."

Who: Jamie Armstrong

What: This 10-year old boy saved his drowning sister from a neighbor's pool.

When: Macon, Georgia

Where: July 26, 1997

Why/How: After hearing her cries for help, Jamie threw her a float. He pulled her to safety.

The Pride Of Mexico

Begin your study of the rich culture of Mexico by creating a student-generated bulletin board. Start the activity by discussing Mexico's ancient pyramids with your students. Explain that ancient civilizations built these pyramids with terraced or sloping sides and flat tops. The tops were used as platforms for temples which honored their gods. These massive structures required great engineering skill; thousands of workers and millions of stone blocks were used. Share pictures of the great pyramids: the Pyramid of the Sun at Teotihuacán, El Castillo at Chichén Itzá, and the Great Temple of the Aztecs at Tenochtitlán (the site of present-day Mexico City).

Next divide your students into pairs. Give each pair a research topic from the list below, and a copy of the title and paragraph blocks from page 27. After each pair has gathered its information, direct partners to write their research topic on the title block, then record their data on the paragraph block. Have each pair lightly color its blocks gray. Instruct each pair to arrange its blocks on the bulletin board with each title block above its matching paragraph block. Fill in odd spaces with extra colored block patterns to construct a step pyramid like the one pictured below. Finish the pyramid by adding the enlarged temple and stairway patterns from page 27.

Topics:

agriculture	economy	holidays	recreational activities	transportation
arts	education	industry	religion	waterways
climate	family life	landforms	shelter	
clothing	flag	language	tourist attractions	
diet	government	plant and animal life		

Long Live Mexico!

Much of Mexico's history and culture is pictured in its huge, colorful murals. This art form originated with the Mayan culture and has been revived in the last century by such artists as Diego Rivera. Show students photographs of Rivera's works. Discuss which aspects of history, politics, or society he is detailing in each mural. Note his use of large figures and bold colors.

Follow up by dividing students into ten research teams. Assign each team a period of history to research (see the list below). Duplicate page 28. Cut out and distribute the appropriate timeline question card for each group to use as a research guide. Next cover a 30-foot length of wall with white bulletin-board paper. Using a pencil, divide the paper into ten three-foot sections. Assign each group a section based on the period in history it researched. Instruct each group to transform the information it gathered into a scene that will be part of a large mural of Mexico's history (see the two sample sections at left). Remind the group to use large figures and bold colors. Tell the group to incorporate its timeline information into the picture so that it becomes part of its mural scene. Finally have the groups connect their sections with colors so that each scene flows into the next one. Title the mural "Long Live Mexico!" and have each group share its work of art.

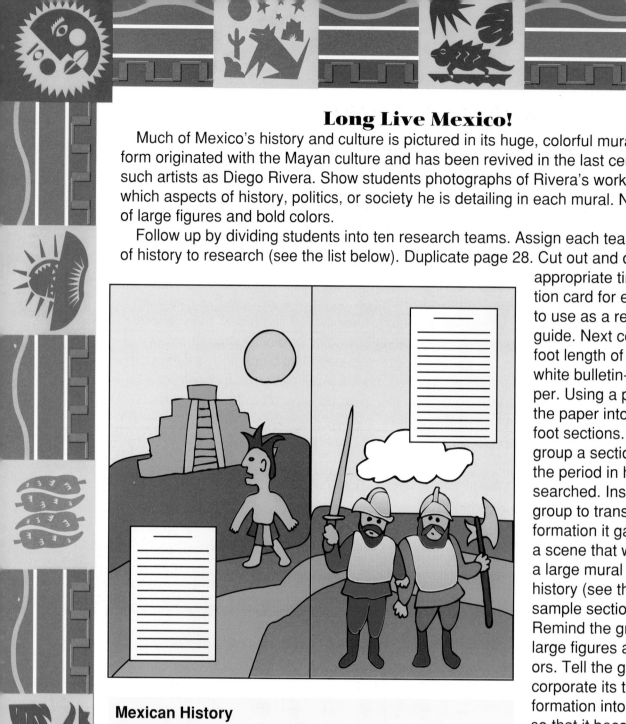

Mexican History

The Mayan Civilization: 250–900
The Toltec Empire: 900–1200
The Aztec Empire: 1400–1521
The Spanish Conquer Mexico: 1519–1521
Mexico Wins Independence From Spain: 1821
Mexico Fights In The Mexican War: 1846–1848
Benito Juarez Is Elected And Brings Reform: 1855
The Mexicans Defeat A Large French Army: 1862
Porfirio Diaz Begins Rule As Dictator: 1876
A Revolution Begins Against The Diaz Government: 1910

Hacky Sack® Footbag

Mexican children enjoy many of the same games and activities that children all over the world enjoy. Footbag is a popular, modern American version of an ancient sport played in North America. It calls for quickness, super-sharp reflexes, and concentration as players stand in a circle and "hack" a small sack or ball. To play the game, have students stand about one foot apart from each other in a circle. Begin the game by tossing the ball up in the air. Direct players to pass the ball back and forth and around the circle using any part of their bodies but their hands. The object of the game is to keep the ball in the air for as long as possible, without allowing it to hit the ground.

Have each student make her own footbag. Give each student a copy of the pattern on page 26, one 7" x 7" square of felt, a 36" length of yarn, one large-eyed needle, about 1/2 cup of popcorn kernels or dried beans, and a pair of scissors. Copy and distribute the directions below for each student.

Directions For The Student:

1. Use a pencil to lightly trace the pattern onto the felt.
2. Cut out the pattern.
3. Thread the needle with the yarn and tie a knot at one end.
4. Stitch together sides A and B from the outer tip to the base. Then continue to stitch, connecting sides C and D, then E and F. Do not tie off the yarn.
5. Holding the stitched sides of the bag in one hand, carefully fill the bag with beans; then stitch together sides G and H.
6. Tie a knot at the base of the yarn. Cut off the excess yarn.

A Taste Of Mexico

Food is always central to a Mexican celebration or fiesta. Fresh fish, meats, grains, fruits, and vegetables are used in a variety of Mexican dishes. Introduce your students to a taste of Mexico by preparing and sharing the following recipes:

Sopaipillas

Although corn has been the most important crop for Mexicans for thousands of years, wheat is also used to make all kinds of cakes, pastries, and sweet breads. Sopaipillas may be served as a bread with a meal. They may also be glazed with honey or dusted with a cinnamon-sugar mixture and served as a dessert. The following recipe makes three to four dozen sopaipillas:

4 cups flour
2 tsp. baking powder
1 tsp. salt
4 Tbsp. shortening
1 1/2 cups warm water
shortening
honey or sugar-cinnamon mixture
powdered sugar

Combine the dry ingredients in a medium-size mixing bowl and cut in the shortening. Make a well in the center of the dry ingredients. Add water and work into a dough. Knead the dough until it is smooth. Then cover it and set it aside for 20 minutes. Heat two inches of shortening in a heavy pan at medium heat. On a lightly floured board, roll the dough to a 1/8-inch thickness. Cut the dough into four-inch squares and fry the squares, turning once, until they are golden on both sides. (Sopaipillas should puff and become hollow after being placed in the heated shortening.) Drain sopaipillas on absorbent towels. Glaze with honey or sugar-cinnamon mixture. Sprinkle with powdered sugar.

Mexican Smoothie

Cold drinks are an important part of the Mexican diet because of the warm climate. Sometimes fruits are blended with milk to create a nutritious drink we call a smoothie.

To make one smoothie, you need:

1 ripe banana, peeled
8 oz. cold milk
1 tablespoon honey
3 drops vanilla extract
2 pinches ground cinnamon

Place all ingredients except the cinnamon into a blender. Cover and blend the ingredients until smooth. Pour the mixture into a glass. Top with cinnamon and serve.

Spanish Word Bank

Spanish is the official language of Mexico. Help your students recognize that many words in the English language originated in Mexico. Examples include: *canyon, patio, plaza,* and *chocolate.* Cover a shoebox with bulletin-board paper, decorate it with symbols of Mexico, and label it "Spanish Word Bank." Cut a 2 1/2-inch opening in the top of the box. Next make multiple copies of the pattern below; then cut out each coin. Challenge your students to identify other Spanish words that have become part of our language. As a student identifies a word, have him fill out the information on one of the coins and deposit the coin in the word bank. At the end of each week, draw several coins from the bank and share the words. Reward each student who contributed a word to the bank.

Spanish word: _____

Meaning: _____

Student name: _____

Spanish word: _____

Meaning: _____

Student name: _____

Spanish word: _____

Meaning: _____

Student name: _____

Spanish word: _____

Meaning: _____

Student name: _____

Spanish word: _____

Meaning: _____

Student name: _____

Spanish word: _____

Meaning: _____

Student name: _____

Patterns

Use with "Courage Under Fire" on page 20.

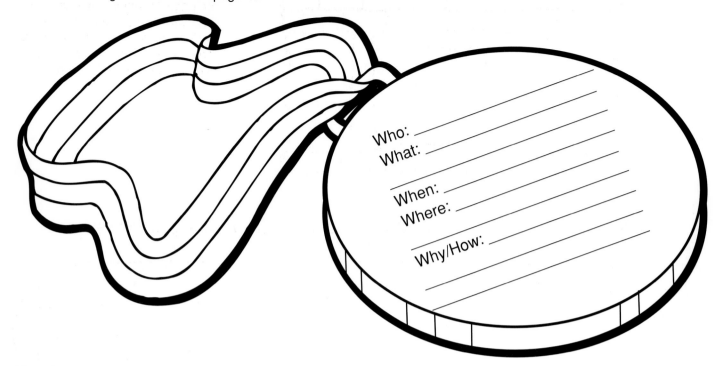

Who: _____
What: _____

When: _____
Where: _____

Why/How: _____

Use with "Hacky Sack® Footbag" on page 23.

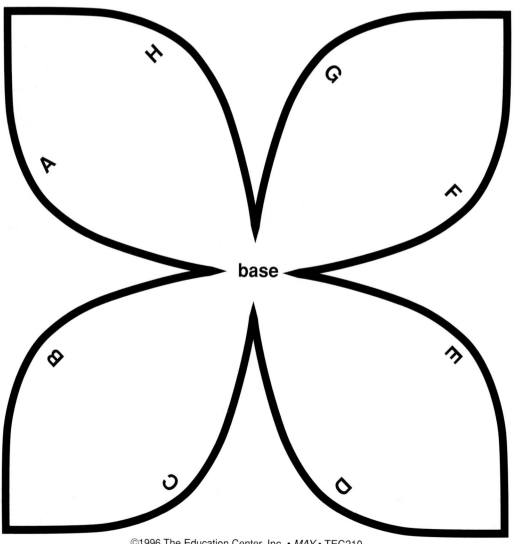

base

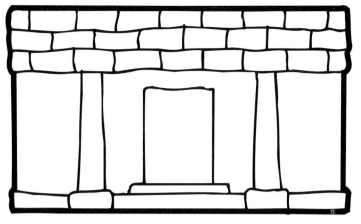

Temple

Patterns

Use with "The Pride Of Mexico" on page 21. Enlarge one temple and one staircase pattern for the bulletin board. Copy and distribute one title block and one paragraph block to each pair of students.

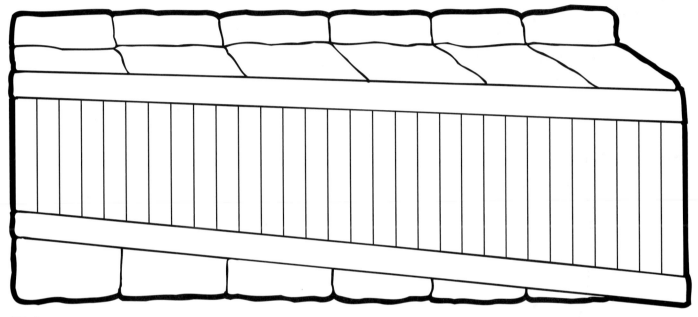

Staircase

Title Block

Paragraph Block

Timeline
Question Cards

250–900

The Mayan Civilization is at its peak.

1. Who were the Maya?
2. Where did the Maya live?
3. What were some of the unique characteristics of the Maya?

1846–1848

Mexico fights in the Mexican War.

1. Who did Mexico fight against?
2. Why did the war occur?
3. What were the results of the war?

900–1200

The Toltec Empire is at its peak.

1. Who were the Toltecs?
2. Where did the Toltecs live?
3. What were some of the unique characteristics of the Toltecs?

1855

Benito Juarez is elected and brings about reform.

1. Who was Benito Juarez?
2. When was he elected president of Mexico?
3. What were the reforms he brought about?

1400–1521

The Aztec Empire is at its peak.

1. Who were the Aztecs?
2. Where did the Aztecs live?
3. What were some of the unique characteristics of the Aztecs?

1862

The Mexicans defeat a large French army.

1. When and where did the battle take place?
2. Why did the battle occur?
3. What were the results of the battle?

1519–1521

The Spanish conquer Mexico.

1. Who led the invasion of Mexico?
2. When and where did the invasion take place?
3. What were the results of the conquest?

1876

Porfirio Diaz begins rule as dictator.

1. Who was Porfirio Diaz?
2. How long was he in office?
3. What were the results of his being in office?

1821

Mexico wins independence from Spain.

1. Who led the revolution against Spain?
2. How long did the revolution last?
3. What were the results of the revolution?

1910

A revolution begins against the Diaz government.

1. Who was involved in the revolution?
2. Why did the revolution occur?
3. What were the results of the revolution?

Note To The Teacher: Duplicate this page to use with "Long Live Mexico!" on page 22. Cut out the cards and give one card to each group of students.

Pyramid Puzzles

Find the hidden word at the base of each Mayan temple. Start with the letter given at the top of the pyramid. As you move down to the next level, add one letter each time to create a new word. You may need to change the order of the letters in the level to create a word. When you get to the base level, you should have a word that relates to Mexico. On the back of the sheet, write a brief explanation of how the word relates to Mexico. Follow the example below.

Example:

a
h a
h a t

A hat, or *sombrero,* is worn by many Mexicans.

1. s

1. _____

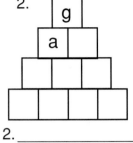

2. g
a

2. _____
_____

3. m

3. _____
_____

4. t
r

4. _____
_____

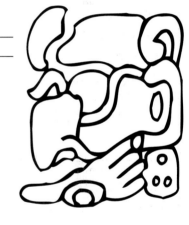

6. s
k

6. _____
_____

5. o
t

5. _____
_____

7. a
n

7. _____
_____

8. p
i

8. _____
_____

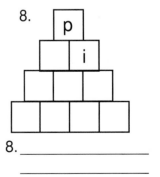

Bonus Box: Use the back of this page to create five more pyramid puzzles. Challenge a classmate to solve them.

Making Mother's Day Memorable

Mothers—they give of themselves in countless ways. With Mother's Day annually falling on the second Sunday in May, use these activities to help your students express their appreciation and create a memorable holiday for the person in their lives whom they call *Mother*.

by Mary Lou Schlosser

From Mommy To Mom

Nothing compares to a mother's love. Share with your students the story *Love You Forever* by Robert Munsch (Firefly Books, 1986) and discuss its theme: Our relationships with our mothers change over time. Ask students: "How has your relationship with your mother changed over the years? Have you seen this happen with your older brothers and sisters? How do you think your mother feels about your growing up?"

Encourage each student to bring in two pictures of himself with his mother—one picture taken when he was very young and one current picture. Have each student cut out two heart shapes from red construction paper. Instruct the student to tape each photograph onto one of the cutouts. Then tell the student to write a caption on each heart below the photograph. The caption should explain what is happening in the photograph and why it is special to him. Divide a bulletin board in half and post the student–mother photographs on the appropriate sides of the board as shown. Invite each student to share his special memories of his mother.

Generous Jars

Here's the next-best thing to bottled love. Have each student create a treat jar that sends her mother a clear message. First brainstorm a list of small-sized snacks that could fit into a baby-food jar, such as Life-saver® candies; M&M's®; or salted, shelled peanuts. Next challenge students to think of a love message that would go with each treat such as "Mom, you are a lifesaver!" or "I'm nuts about you, Mom!" Have each student choose a message and the treat to fill the jar she will send. Copy and distribute the directions below for each student. Then give each student a clean baby-food jar (with the label removed), a 3" x 2" strip of paper, a 4" x 4" piece of colorful fabric, a 14-inch length of ribbon, pinking shears, a hole puncher, glue, a colored pencil, and enough snack food to fill the small jar.

Directions:
Step 1: Use pinking shears to cut a circle of fabric about 1 1/2 inches larger than the outside edge of the jar lid. Apply a light layer of glue to the top of the jar lid; then center the circle of fabric and glue it to the lid.
Step 2: Fold the paper strip to make a card. Hole-punch the top left corner. Write your message to your mother on the inside of the card.
Step 3: Put the ribbon through the hole in the card; then tie the ribbon to the outer rim of the jar lid.
Step 4: Fill the jar with treats and secure the lid.

Heartfelt Words

Help students capture their thoughts— and their mothers' hearts. Display the list of sentence starters below. Have each student cut out a large heart from a 12" x 18" piece of paper, then write in the center, "My Heart Belongs To Mom." During freetime, instruct the student to copy several sentence starters onto his heart and complete each thought by writing directly on the heart cutout. Direct the student to use both the front and back of the heart for his entries. When his sentences are complete, instruct the student to decorate the heart and sign his name. When these messages of love are given to moms, hearts will melt.

My favorite memory of Mom is…
Important events in my mom's life include…
The funniest thing my mom ever did was…
The best way I can show Mom I care is…
If I could treat my mom to a shopping spree, I know she would like…
If I had to compare my mom to a famous person, it would be _____ because…
Things my mom often tells me to do are…
Things my mom often tells me not to do are…
If I could take my mom any place in the world, it would be _____ because…
Things I could do to make life a little easier for my mom include…
I love my mom because…

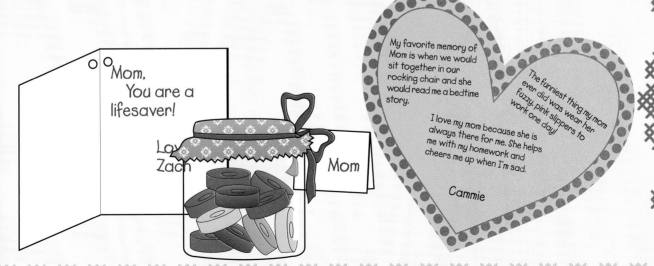

31

Mothers Throughout The Years

Help each student discover more about herself by investigating the history of the mothers, grandmothers, and great-grandmothers in her family. Begin by discussing the ways that students can gather information about their relatives, such as leafing through a family photo album, researching a genealogy chart, interviewing family members, or writing to relatives for information. Next have each student select one mother from her family to research. Encourage the student to use any of the resources listed above to find out about this mother. Duplicate page 34 for each student to use for recording her research. After reviewing the questions on the page, encourage each student to add additional questions to the sheet.

If photos of this mother are available, have the student get permission to bring them in for the project. Photocopy the pictures so that she can take the originals home.

After each student has completed page 34, have her compile her research and photos, along with any other keepsakes, into an album about this mother. Supply various colors of 9" x 12" construction paper, scissors, glue, and markers to make the album pages; and brads, yarn, or ribbon to bind the album. Instruct the student to rewrite the gathered information onto separate sheets of notepaper. Then instruct her to glue each sheet of notepaper and each photograph onto a separate piece of colored paper. (If no photograph is available, direct the student to draw a picture of her relative based on the information she gathered.) Instruct the student to decorate each page with symbols or pictures that illustrate this mother's life. Have the student arrange the pages. Then direct her to add front and back album covers and bind them all together. Have the student title her book "A Mother's Day Family Album: A Tribute To [mother's name]."

Humor Me...I'm A Mom!

Use wit from the funnies to motivate your students' creative thinking. Duplicate a supply of "Merry Moms In Comical Cartoons" on page 35. Collect and cut out a variety of newspaper cartoons that feature mothers. Glue each cartoon into a separate file folder and put a copy of page 35 in each folder. Store the folders at a center. When a student has free time, direct him to choose a cartoon folder, then complete page 35 and hand it in. Once every student has had a chance to read and respond to a cartoon, display the cartoons and student response sheets for all to enjoy.

Personalized Gift Wrap

Wrap the Mother's Day creations made in this unit with personalized gift wrap. Supply each student with a large sheet of newsprint paper; a small, dry sponge; scissors; a marker; and stencil paints of various colors. Instruct each student to draw a simple design onto his sponge with the marker, and then cut out the resulting stencil.

Next pour several colors of paint into different plastic lids. Instruct each student to choose one color to use with his stencil. Direct him to lightly dip his sponge into the paint, then blot the excess paint onto a scrap of paper before sponge-painting his paper. If a student wishes to use a different color of paint, inform him that he must use a stencil that is assigned to that color. Encourage students to try other stencils to vary their designs. After the paper has dried overnight, have each student add drawings or personal messages to the paper. Finally have the student use the paper to wrap his mother's gift. If your class has created several Mother's Day projects, vary the idea by having the student decorate a large, brown paper bag as a gift bag.

Mother's Tea

End your month of Mother's Day activities by hosting a special tea party for the mothers or honored guests of your students. Divide students into groups; then assign each group a task for organizing the party. Suggested group assignments include: addressing and mailing invitations, planning and setting up decorations, setting the table and arranging the place settings, providing the entertainment, and cleaning up. Purchase the tea as well as the eating utensils. If desired, have the students help you make treats to serve, such as cookies or cakes.

On the day of the tea, have one or two students (perhaps those who will not have visitors) greet each guest as she arrives and show her to her seat. When all the guests have arrived, have the students perform a special Mother's Day song, poem, or reading. Have each student present the gift(s) he created during the month to his honored guest. If desired, take a photo of each student with his guest. Once they're developed, display the photos. Then have each student write a note to his guest and enclose the photograph as a keepsake of the special day.

Portrait Of A Mother

Name of person being investigated: _____

Relationship to me: _____

How I conducted my research: _____

_____

Date of birth: _____

Place of birth: _____

Maiden name: _____

Husband's name: _____

Date of marriage: _____

Place of marriage: _____

Children's names: _____

Hobbies/interests: _____

What has this person enjoyed most about being a mother? _____

_____

What has this person enjoyed least about being a mother? _____

_____

What advice would this person give future mothers about rearing children?

_____

_____

What is this person's favorite Mother's Day memory? _____

_____

_____

Other questions: _____

_____

_____

©1996 The Education Center, Inc. • *MAY* • TEC210

Merry Moms In Comical Cartoons

What's so funny about being a mom? Find out by looking at motherhood through the eyes of a cartoon writer. Select a cartoon to read. Then write or draw your answers about the cartoon mom in the boxes below.

Cartoon title:

Cartoon mom's name:
(If she doesn't have a name, what name would you give her?)

Five words that describe this cartoon mom:

Description of other family members in this cartoon (including pets):

The greatest thing about being this cartoon mom is:

The worst thing about being this cartoon mom is:

If this cartoon mom were being interviewed, she would say that a mother is:

One situation it would be funny to see this cartoon mom in is:

If *my* mom were the mom in this cartoon:

Bonus Box: Write and illustrate a cartoon starring your mom and other members of your family.

Note To The Teacher: Use this page with "Humor Me… I'm A Mom!" on page 32.

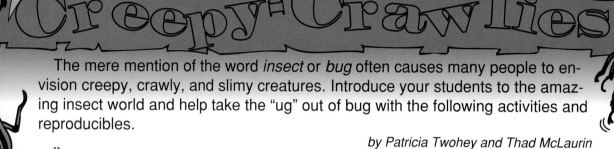

Creepy-Crawlies

The mere mention of the word *insect* or *bug* often causes many people to envision creepy, crawly, and slimy creatures. Introduce your students to the amazing insect world and help take the "ug" out of bug with the following activities and reproducibles.

by Patricia Twohey and Thad McLaurin

Backyard Bugs

Bugs—they are everywhere. You see them circling a lamppost, crawling across the sidewalk, and buzzing through the air. Instruct each student to spend a weekend locating and observing the bugs that live in his backyard or around his home. Direct him to select one bug to research following these instructions:

Directions To The Student:

1. Take an instant photo, sketch a picture, or photocopy a picture of the bug from a magazine or book.
2. Research the following information about the insect: common name, description of body features, whether or not the bug is an insect, where you found this bug, what this bug eats, life span of the bug, and other interesting facts.
3. Summarize your information in a brief paragraph about the insect on a 3 1/2" x 5" index card. (If you do not have resources at home, wait and research the bug at school.)

Display the bug pictures and index cards on a bulletin board as shown above. Enlarge, duplicate, and have a student volunteer color the bug patterns on page 42; then arrange the patterns around the title as shown. Have each student point out his bug on the board and read the information on his index card. Encourage students to add more bugs and insects to the board as they are discovered throughout the unit.

Lunch At McInsect's

Insect mouths come in a variety of shapes and sizes, and have special equipment to allow the insect to feed. Generally an insect either sucks its food up through a strawlike apparatus or chews it. Help students discover these and other facts about insect eating habits with the following activity: Duplicate one copy of page 43 for every two students. Then list the following insect names on the board:

bee	ant	beetle	cricket	grasshopper
fruit fly	cicada	flea	moth	dragonfly
termite	ladybug	mosquito	hornet	praying mantis

Next divide the students into pairs and assign each pair one of the insects listed on the board. Instruct each pair to research the eating habits of its insect, then complete the reproducible on page 43. Tell each pair to include a detailed drawing of its insect, an up-close drawing of the insect's mouth, information on how it eats, and information on what it eats. Direct each pair to create an imaginative meal for its insect as it might appear on a menu. For example: *Butterfly Bisque—a tasty blend of nectars made from a variety of colorful flowers and served in an orchid for your tasting pleasure.* Fold a large sheet of light-colored paper in half to create a giant menu. Encourage each pair to write the description of its unique meal on the menu, then illustrate the meal underneath the description. Label the front of the menu "Bodacious Bug Bistro" and display for all to enjoy.

Incredible!

Yuck!

Insect Opinion Poll

Although insects—the largest animal group—are often very beneficial to humans, they are not very popular. Have your students explore the differing opinions people have about insects by conducting an "Insect Opinion Poll." Duplicate page 44 for each student. Then ask the class to predict if more people like or dislike insects. Also have each student predict which insect on the poll will be the most popular. Instruct each student to survey ten people—other than his classmates—and create a bar graph of the results as directed on the reproducible. On the blackboard, tally the results from each student's poll. Give each student a sheet of white paper on which to make a bar graph depicting the results of the class tally. Display the bar graphs on a bulletin board or wall. Then have students answer the following questions: "Were your predictions of the most popular insect correct? What generalizations can be drawn from the results? What reasons can explain the results? Do the class bar-graph results differ from your opinion-poll bar graph? How did the results compare to the class's prediction? Would the results be the same if a different group were surveyed?"

Arthropods, Insects, And Bugs— Is There A Difference!

Many people refer to most *arthropods* as "bugs." What they don't realize is that *true bugs* actually belong to a unique order of insects known as *Hemiptera.* Help your students distinguish between the various hierarchies of arthropods with the following activity:

Gather several resource books that include information and pictures of the arthropods listed on page 45. Duplicate page 45 for each student. Instruct the student to classify each animal listed by researching and completing the chart. After discussing the chart as a class, have each student use his knowledge of bugs and insects to illustrate a fictitious arthropod on the back of his page. As each student presents his creation to the rest of the class, have him explain how his creation fits into the category of an insect, bug, or some other type of arthropod.

Hmmm... dinner ought to be a "chinch!"

All In The Family

Most insects have no family life. However, social insects—such as ants, bees, termites, and wasps—live in highly organized colonies in which every member has a role to play in the survival of the colony. Help students learn about these orderly insects with the following group collaboration:

Divide the class into eight groups and assign two groups to each of the following social insects: ants, bees, termites, and wasps. Have each group answer the following questions using reference materials:

- Describe the physical appearance of your insect in detail.
- What roles do the *queen, nurses, workers,* and *soldiers* play in your insect colony?
- Describe your colony's *habitat* (home).
- How does the colony deal with sick members?
- How does the colony gather food?
- What type of food does the colony eat?
- How does the colony deal with overcrowding?
- What dangers face your colony, and how does it protect itself?
- How does the colony deal with waste?
- How is this insect beneficial or harmful to humans?

Instruct each group to prepare a unique presentation of its facts (see list below). After each group has presented its information, have the class discuss the similarities and differences among the four types of insects researched.

- Present a group skit in which each member plays a different role in an insect colony.
- Write and perform a rap that shares facts about the insect group.
- Create a model of the insect habitat, including figures representing each colony member.
- Collaborate on a story about a colony that is being threatened. Bring in facts about the various roles and responsibilities of colony members by describing how each reacts in response to the threat.

Chomp!
Chomp!

Joyful Noise

Joyful Noise: Poems For Two Voices by Paul Fleischman (HarperCollins Children's Books, 1988) contains a unique collection of insect poetry. The poetry is unusual in that certain lines are read by only one reader, whereas other lines are read in unison. This unique way of reading poetry produces insect sounds that are almost musical.

Help your students experience this joyful noise. Divide students into pairs; then assign each pair a poem from *Joyful Noise: Poems For Two Voices*. Allow time for each pair to learn and rehearse its poem. Schedule a time one morning or afternoon for each pair to perform its poem for the rest of the class. Be sure to invite parents to this special reading.

As an extension activity, have each pair write an original poem about insects using this unique and musical format.

Insect Trivia Comic Books

Take advantage of children's fondness for comics by having each student research unbelievable facts about insects, then present the information in comic book form. Have each student use the steps below to construct his comic book. To extend the activity, duplicate "Insect Trivia Trek" on page 46 for each student to complete.

Materials For Each Student: five 8 1/2" x 11" sheets of white paper, one 8 1/2" x 11" sheet of colored construction paper, markers, crayons, access to a stapler

Step 1: Stack the five sheets of white paper; then fold in half widthwise as shown.
Step 2: Fold the colored sheet of construction paper in half widthwise; then insert the folded stack of white paper into the folded colored sheet as shown.
Step 3: Bind the book by stapling along the fold as shown.
Step 4: Create a title for the cover of your book.
Step 5: Create one cartoon per page and include a caption explaining each cartoon.
Step 6: Be prepared to present your Insect Trivia Comic Book to your classmates.

Step 1　　　　**Steps 2, 3, and 4**

Rayna's Cool Insect Trivia Book

Some ants can lift objects that are 50 times the weight of their bodies.

Step 5

Tri-Fold Insect Reports

Here's a simple and clever tool for helping students through the research and report-writing process. Duplicate a class supply of the "Insect Research Organizer" on page 47. Instruct each student to select an unfamiliar insect, then use the organizer to help her gather research on her insect. After a student has completed her research and organized her facts, instruct her to use the steps below to create a tri-fold insect report. Display each tri-fold report around the classroom or in the media center; then schedule an evening for students to present their reports to parents.

As a follow-up activity, have each student use the displayed reports and other reference materials to complete the "Insect Name Game" on page 48.

Materials For Each Student: one 12" x 18" sheet of colored construction paper, one 3" x 3" piece of white paper, one 1" x 14" strip of colored construction paper, one 1/2" x 6" strip of colored construction paper, glue, markers, access to a stapler, tape (optional)

Directions To The Student:
1. Fold the large sheet of paper into thirds widthwise. Use a marker to draw a vertical line through each fold as shown.
2. Next draw a horizontal line through the middle of the paper as shown to make six boxes.
3. Label the top of each box with one of the six research topics on your "Insect Research Organizer."
4. Use the notes in each section of your organizer to create one or two paragraphs of information for each box.
5. Add pictures, graphs, or illustrations to each box.
6. Write your name on the center of the 1" x 14" strip of paper.
7. Staple the left-hand end of the 1" x 14" strip to the upper left-hand end of the tri-fold; then staple the right-hand end of the 1" x 14" strip to the upper right-hand end of the tri-fold as shown.
8. Staple or tape the 1/2" x 6" strip to the center of the 1" x 14" strip so that it hangs down in the center of the tri-fold as shown.
9. Use markers to draw a picture of your insect on the 3" x 3" piece of white paper. Cut out and staple the illustration to the end of the 1/2" x 6" strip as shown.

40

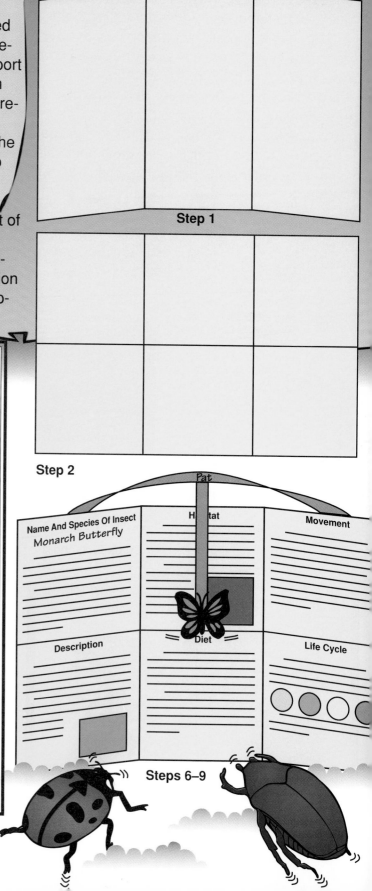

Step 1

Step 2

Name And Species Of Insect
Monarch Butterfly

Habitat

Movement

Description

Diet

Life Cycle

Steps 6–9

Insect Architects

What better way to assess each student's knowledge of insects than by having him design and build an insect. Send a note home a week before beginning this project requesting art supplies such as paper cups, toilet paper and paper-towel rolls, craft sticks, pipe cleaners, buttons, glitter, scrap material, balloons, empty plastic bottles, and hot glue dispensers. Also recruit a couple of parent volunteers to help distribute art supplies the day of the activity.

Before beginning the project, have students review the physical characteristics of an insect. Then instruct each student to design and construct an insect that has these body parts—head, thorax, abdomen, and six jointed legs. Have the student add color to his insect. Then display the insects for all to enjoy or use them to complete "Insect Tales" below.

Insect Tales

Have your students use the models they created in "Insect Architects" above with the following five-day creative-writing activity:

Day One: Instruct each student to choose one insect model. (The student doesn't have to select his own model.) Then list the following questions on the board:

- What is the size of your insect?
- Does it have any special colors or camouflage?
- Does it have special body parts such as wings, stingers, or antennae?
- How does it move around?
- What does it eat?
- Where does it live?
- Is it helpful, or is it a pest?
- What are its enemies?

Have each student brainstorm answers to these questions related to the insect she has chosen.

Day Two: Next have the student write the first draft of a story that describes a typical day in the life of her insect.

Days Three and Four: Meet with each author to listen to, talk about, and edit her insect tale.

Day Five: Have each student complete the final copy of her insect tale by hand or on a computer. Encourage the student to include original illustrations.

Schedule a day for each student to read her insect tale to the rest of the class. Then post the tales on a bulletin board for others to read.

How It Eats:

_____
_____
_____
_____
_____
_____
_____

What It Eats:

_____
_____
_____
_____
_____
_____
_____

(Name Of Insect)

(Detailed Drawing Of Insect)

(Up-Close Drawing Of Insect's Mouth)

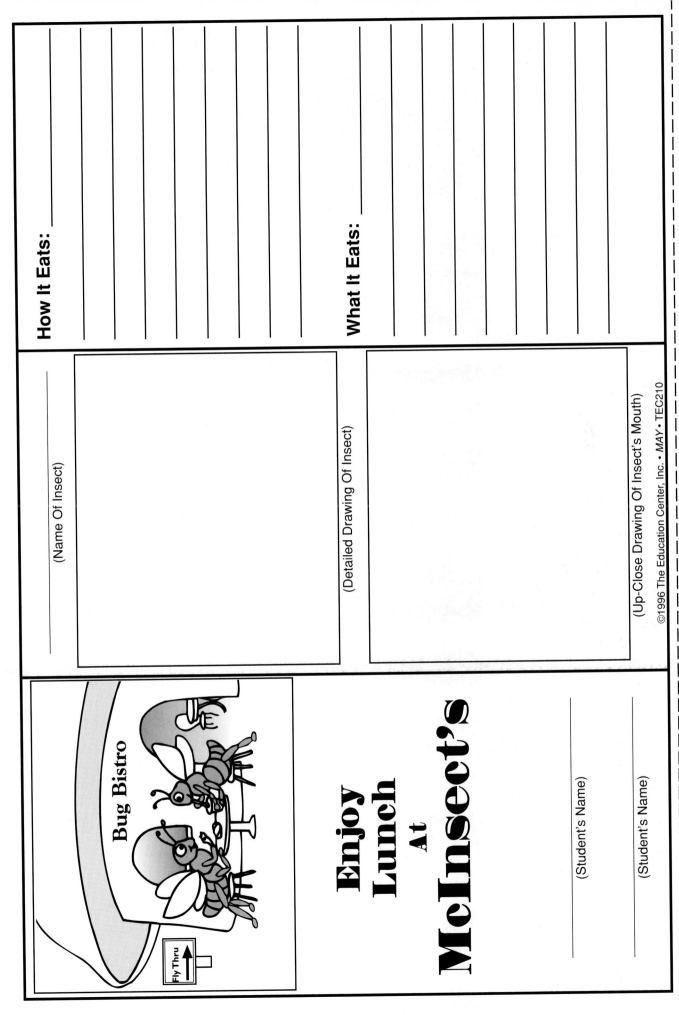

Bug Bistro

Fly Thru

Enjoy Lunch At McInsect's

(Student's Name)

(Student's Name)

Note To The Teacher: Duplicate this page for each pair of students and use with "Lunch At McInsect's" on page 37.

44

Conducting an opinion poll, making a bar graph

Insect Opinion Poll

I'm musically talented!

Do people like insects? Which insects do they like or dislike? Ask ten people to complete the opinion poll below. Tally the totals at the bottom of each column. Use your results to make a bar graph on the back of this page. What conclusions can you make based on your bar graph?

Name Of Person Being Polled	Do You Like (L) Or Dislike (D) These Insects?												What Is Your Favorite Insect?	What Is Your Least Favorite Insect?
	Ant		Cockroach		Cricket		Butterfly		Mosquito		Bee			
	L	D	L	D	L	D	L	D	L	D	L	D		
1.														
2.														
3.														
4.														
5.														
6.														
7.														
8.														
9.														
10.														
Totals														

I'm so beautiful!

I'm a pest!

I'm so sweet!

I love picnics!

Bonus Box: On the back of this page, list several reasons why you think certain insects on your poll are liked and others are disliked.

©1996 The Education Center, Inc. • *MAY* • TEC210

Note To The Teacher: Duplicate this page for each student and use with "Insect Opinion Poll" on page 37.

Arthropods → Insects → Bugs

Arthropods are animals that have *exoskeletons* (outer protective shells) and jointed legs. Arthropods include *insects, arachnids, crustaceans, diplopods,* and *chilopods.* An insect has six jointed legs and a three-sectioned body consisting of a *head, thorax,* and *abdomen.* Most people don't realize that *true bugs* actually belong to a unique order of insects known as *Hemiptera.* Bugs do not have teeth or chewing mouth parts. Instead bugs have horny, jointed beaks used for piercing and sucking. When resting, a bug's back wings are covered by the front wings, which have a leathery or hard base.

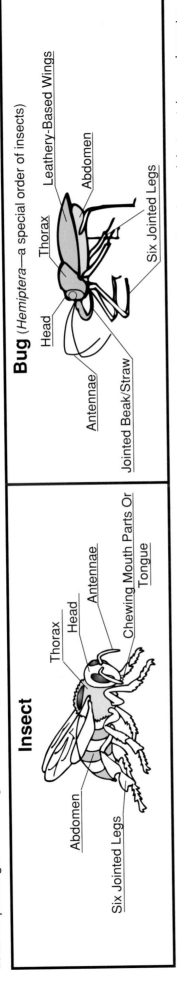

Insect

Thorax
Head
Antennae
Chewing Mouth Parts Or Tongue
Abdomen
Six Jointed Legs

Bug (*Hemiptera*—a special order of insects)

Head
Thorax
Leathery-Based Wings
Abdomen
Six Jointed Legs
Antennae
Jointed Beak/Straw

Directions: Research the characteristics for the arthropods listed at the top of each column. Check the box below each arthropod that matches a character-istic of that animal. In the last box put an "I" if the arthropod is an insect, a "B" if the arthropod is a bug, and an "O" if it is a different type of arthropod. (Be careful. Don't let names fool you.)

Characteristics	Praying Mantis	Ladybug	Cockroach	Water Bug	Spider	Butterfly	Tick	Centipede	Bee	Chinch Bug
Three Body Parts (Head, Thorax, Abdomen)										
Six Jointed Legs										
Jointed Beak Or Straw For Sucking Liquids										
Chewing Mouth Parts And/Or Sucking Tongue										
Leathery-Based Wings										
I = Insect B = Bug O = Other Kind Of Arthropod										

Note To The Teacher: Duplicate this page for each student and use with "Arthropods, Insects, And Bugs—Is There A Difference?" on page 38.

Insect Trivia Trek

Learn some interesting and amazing insect trivia and polish up on your problem-solving skills by answering the following questions:

1. Scientists have identified more than 1,500,000 species of animals. About 1,000,000 of the identified species are insects. Approximately what fraction of the identified species are insects?

2. Scientists discover about 10,000 new species of insects each year. How many new insects will be discovered in ten years? In 100 years?

3. Even though most insects are small, many have incredible strength. If a honeybee were the size of a man, it could pull a 30-ton truck by itself! Many ants can lift things 50 times their own weight. Multiply your weight by 50. Write the answer. Can you lift that much weight?

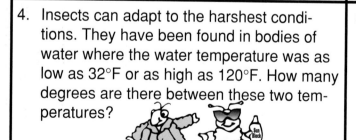

4. Insects can adapt to the harshest conditions. They have been found in bodies of water where the water temperature was as low as 32°F or as high as 120°F. How many degrees are there between these two temperatures?

5. A dragonfly's flight speed can reach 60 miles per hour. How long would it take a dragonfly to travel 100 miles at top speed?

6. A housefly beats its wings about 200 times per second! How many times does a housefly beat its wings in one day?

7. Many insects have incredible reproductive ability. For example, some queen termites can lay up to 30,000 eggs a day. If the queen continued laying eggs at this rate each day, how many eggs would she lay in one year?

8. Some beetles can carry items weighing 850 times their own weight. If a woman weighing 125 pounds could proportionally carry as much weight as a beetle, how much could she carry?

Bonus Box: Less than one percent of the estimated 1,000,000 species of insects are harmful. Only a few hundred of the thousands of insect species found in the United States are serious pests. List on the back of this page as many insects as you can that cause serious damage to crops, homes, or people.

©1996 The Education Center, Inc. • MAY • TEC210 • Key p. 95

Note To The Teacher: Duplicate for each student and use as an extension activity to accompany "Insect Trivia Comic Books" on page 39.

Insect Research Organizer

Use this page to organize your insect research. Use as many different resource and reference books as possible to collect information for each topic listed below. Write the facts you collect in note form, not in complete sentences. Create a bibliography on the back of this page of each resource used in your research. Be sure to include the *title, author's name,* and *page number(s)*.

Name And Species Of Insect
What is the insect's scientific name and common name? What is its species?

Habitat
Where does the insect live? What does it use to make its home?

Movement
How does it move around? How fast does it move?

Description
What does it look like? What is its size, color, and shape?

Diet
What does it eat? How much does it eat?

Life Cycle
How many stages does it experience? What is the average life span of this insect? _____

Note To The Teacher: Duplicate a class supply of this page to use with "Tri-Fold Insect Reports" on page 40. Provide students with access to research materials in the classroom and media center.

Name_____ *Research, vocabulary*

Insect Name Game

Place the name of one insect in each box below that has that particular characteristic. Once an insect's name is written in a box, that name cannot be used again. Be sure to spell the insect's name correctly.

Has compound eyes.	Tastes with its legs.	Has long antennae.	Has two wings.	Is a great jumper.
Sucks food through a tube.	Has chewing mouth parts.	Is useful to humans.	Is a pest to humans.	Is a pest to plants.
Experiences complete metamorphosis.	Experiences incomplete metamorphosis.	Is a social insect.	Lays more than 100 eggs at a time.	Spends part of its life in water.
Eats wood.	Uses a stinger.	Makes a musical sound.	Builds a nest.	Carries diseases.
Crawls.	Has unusual antennae.	Is good at camouflaging itself.	Has hard, sharp, pincher-like jaws.	Looks colorful.

Bonus Box: Congratulations, you've completed the "Insect Name Game." Now for the *real* challenge. Add a second insect to each box. Remember, the insect name cannot already appear on the page. If you succeed, you can really call yourself a junior entomologist!

Note To The Teacher: Duplicate this page for each student. Provide reference materials and/or have students use information from the tri-fold insect reports from page 40 to complete the game.

Metamorphosis

Metamorphosis refers to a change in body form or appearance. Insects such as bees, butterflies, fleas, and ants all experience *complete metamorphosis* in which the insect develops in four stages: *egg, larva, pupa,* and *adult.* Other insects—such as grasshoppers, cockroaches, and dragonflies—undergo *incomplete metamorphosis* in which the insect develops in three stages: *egg, nymph,* and *adult.*

Research both types of metamorphosis to find out what happens in each stage. Then briefly explain what happens in each stage in the spaces provided. Also color the illustrations for each stage.

Complete Metamorphosis	Incomplete Metamorphosis
Stage 1: Egg	**Stage 1: Egg**
Stage 2: Larva	**Stage 2: Nymph**
Stage 3: Pupa	**Stage 3: Adult**
Stage 4: Adult	

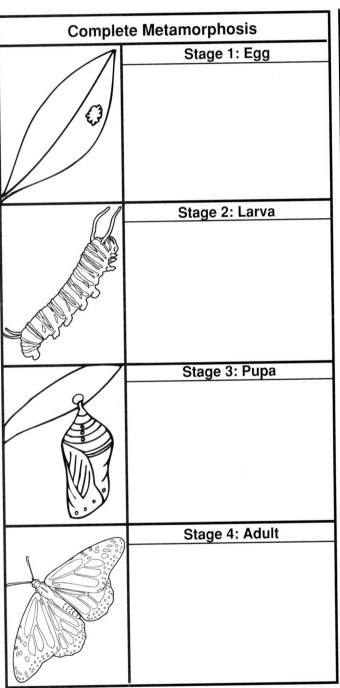
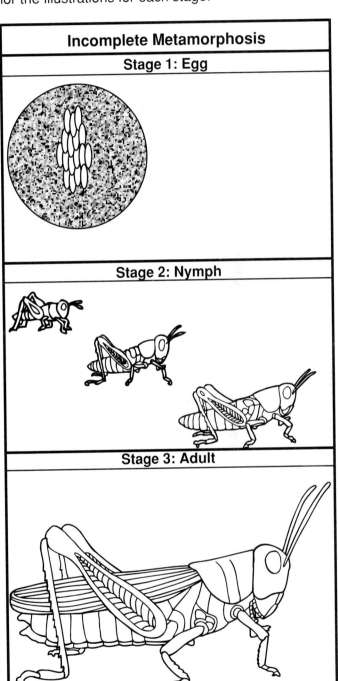

Bonus Box: If you could experience complete metamorphosis, which insect would you want to become and why? Write your response on the back of this page.

- -

Note To The Teacher: Duplicate one copy for each student. Use this reproducible as an extension activity. Provide students with research and reference materials on insects, as well as markers or crayons for coloring the illustrations.

Heralding Our Heroes

While there is no typical mold for a hero, all heroes share some common characteristics. We look to heroes as role models to guide our behavior and to provide standards for our goals. Open your students' eyes to the heroes of the past and present with the creative activities featured in this unit.
by Barbara Samuels, Judith Shutter, Mary Spaulding, and Stephanie Willett-Smith

First-Place Heroes

Create a Hero Hall Of Fame with this fun activity. Provide each student with a copy of the frame pattern on page 58. Ask each student to think of a person whom she considers to be a hero. Remind students that heroes don't necessarily have to be well known. Have each student record the name of her selected hero in the ribbon at the bottom of the frame. Then, on the lines around the frame, instruct the student to record the characteristics and achievements that have made that individual heroic. Complete the activity by having each child draw a picture of her hero inside the frame. If desired, add a trophy cutout (enlarge the one on page 62) to the board as shown. Arrange the finished frames around the trophy on the bulletin board.

Hero Hall Of Fame

Humming A Tune For A Hero

Switch on your radio and you're sure to hear some songs about heroes. Encourage your students to explore heroism by listening to two songs: "Hero" sung by Mariah Carey and "Wind Beneath My Wings" sung by Bette Midler. Instruct students to think about the following questions as they listen to the songs: "Who is the hero in the song? What characteristics make him or her a hero?" Afterwards divide your class into groups of three to four students. Provide each group with a copy of page 59 to complete. Then discuss and record the groups' responses on chart paper to create a list of heroic traits. Display this list in your room for students' reference.

In Search Of Heroes

Expose your students to some unsung heroes with the book *People Who Make A Difference* by Brent Ashabranner (Dutton Children's Books, 1989). Read aloud several selections from the book and have students explain why the featured individuals are viewed as heroes. Ask your students the following questions: "Who can become a hero? Do heroes have to be famous and well known? What does it take to be a hero?" Use this book's four categories of everyday heroes (listed below) as a way to organize a further study of heroes:

1. Helping Those Most In Need Of Help
2. Making A Difference In The Environment
3. Making A Difference Through Community Service
4. Making A Difference By Personal Example

Record each of these headings on a separate piece of chart paper. Post the charts on a wall in your room. Then have your students look through back issues of newspapers and magazines to find examples of stories featuring heroes. As a class, discuss the hero(es) featured in each story. Complete the activity by having your students classify the hero(es) featured in each article into one of the four categories. Then attach the article to the corresponding chart. Your students will be amazed at the number of ordinary people who do extraordinary things in our world!

51

Hero Heraldry

Calling all heroes! Combine your celebration of unsung heroes with the study of *heraldry.* Heraldry is the study of a system of symbols used to represent people, families, countries, or institutions such as churches or universities. One basic symbol of heraldry, the *coat of arms,* originated in the early 1100s when knights fighting in the Crusades needed a method of identification. During battles, knights covered their bodies and heads in metal and could be identified only by the coats of arms displayed on their shields and flags. Then, like today, a *coat of arms* consisted of an insignia or a design that represented the individual, his family, his country, or his church.

Begin by having your students research *heraldry.* Instruct each student to design one of the elements of a coat of arms—the *shield*—to represent the unsung hero he honored in "Heralding Unsung Heroes." Tell the student to decorate his shield with symbols and designs that reveal the personal characteristics of his unsung hero. Then provide each student with a piece of cardboard cut in the shape of a shield similar to one of those pictured on this page. Instruct each student to transfer his designs onto the shield. Invite him to use yarn, cardboard, beads, macaroni, and other craft items to make his designs three-dimensional. Allow each student to share his completed shield at your class's unsung hero reception (see "Heralding Unsung Heroes").

Heralding Unsung Heroes

A hero doesn't have to be famous. In fact, most aren't. Often the most influential person in a child's life is someone she comes in contact with on a daily basis. Teach your students to recognize and appreciate the efforts of the unsung heroes in their lives with the following activity.

Begin by discussing the term *unsung hero*—"a hero who is not celebrated or praised." Ask each student to name and describe an unsung hero who has impacted his life. Have the student explain why this person is important to him. Then direct each child to write a paragraph detailing the importance of his unsung hero. Attach this paragraph to the back of the completed shield described in the art activity in "Hero Heraldry."

Schedule an afternoon reception to honor these unsung heroes. Direct each student to make an invitation and deliver it to his hero. Serve cookies and punch at the reception, and allow each child to share his paragraph and shield with his hero.

Hero Sandwich

Give your students a taste of biographies with this fun activity. Assign each student a specific hero to research (see the list below). Instruct each student to find out about his hero's birthdate and birthplace, early life, education, accomplishments, and heroic deeds. Duplicate one copy of pages 60 and 61 for each student. Then provide each student with the materials listed on page 60. Tell students to follow the directions on page 60. Display their finished biographies on a bulletin board with the title "A Huge Helping Of Heroes."

Heroes For Hero Sandwiches

Abigail Adams	Sam Houston	James Monroe
Maya Angelou	Andrew Jackson	Sandra Day O'Connor
Susan B. Anthony	Thomas Jefferson	Eleanor Roosevelt
Arthur Ashe	Barbara Jordan	Franklin D. Roosevelt
Daniel Boone	Helen Keller	Harriet Tubman
Rachel Carson	John F. Kennedy	Booker T. Washington
George Washington Carver	Martin Luther King, Jr.	George Washington
Amelia Earhart	Abraham Lincoln	Woodrow Wilson
Nathanael Greene	James Madison	

Hometown Heroes

Here's a winning activity to sharpen your students' investigative skills. Have each student recall the hometown of the hero whose biography he wrote for the "Hero Sandwich" activity. Obtain the chamber-of-commerce addresses for each of these hometowns from your local chamber of commerce. Then have each student write a business letter to the chamber of commerce in his hero's hometown asking how the town has commemorated the birth or life of its hero. Have students ask questions such as, "Did the town name a street, building, or school after the hero? Does the town have an annual parade or event in honor of the hero? Is there a tourist attraction in honor of that person?"

Duplicate several copies of the trophy pattern on page 62 for each student. As each response arrives, have the student record the information he receives on his trophy. Ask the student to fill out a separate trophy for each different way his hero is commemorated in his hometown. Then display the information on a graph like the one pictured at right. Plot the methods of tribute on the x-axis and the numbers on the y-axis. The result will be an interesting and informative display.

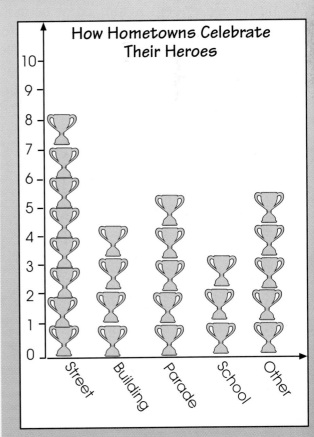

How Hometowns Celebrate Their Heroes

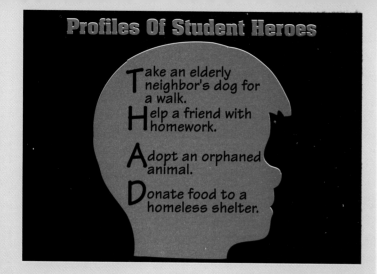

Profiles Of Student Heroes

Take an elderly neighbor's dog for a walk.

Help a friend with homework.

Adopt an orphaned animal.

Donate food to a homeless shelter.

Fin, Feathers, And Fur: Animal Heroes

Expose your students to a new breed of heroes with this activity. Gather a collection of literature in which animals are featured as heroes. Some suggested books include the following:

Charlotte's Web by E. B. White (HarperCollins Children's Books, 1974)

The Incredible Journey by Sheila Burnford (Bantam Books, Inc.; 1985)

Stone Fox by John R. Gardiner (HarperCollins Children's Books, 1983)

Old Yeller by Fred Gipson (HarperCollins Children's Books, 1990)

Black Beauty by Anna Sewell (Random House Books for Young Readers, 1993)

Read one or more of these books to your students. Discuss the heroic deeds of the animals featured. Then ask students to share the names of other heroic animals they have read or heard about in stories, plays, television shows, or movies. Record students' responses on the board and discuss the characteristics that make each of these animals a hero.

Next have each student create an original animal hero of his own. Give each student a supply of modeling clay with which to construct a sculpture of an animal. Have each student mount his animal on a small block of wood along with a plaque bearing the animal's name. Invite the student to write a short story featuring his animal hero in the starring role. Remind the student to include the setting, characters, plot, and solution in his story. Bind these completed stories in a book. Then display the hero sculptures and the book in your media center for others to enjoy.

Profiles Of Student Heroes

Are your students hero wanna-bes? Then help them develop the characteristics that will make them heroes. Discuss many of the everyday actions of ordinary people that are actually heroic. Help students think of ways they can become heroes at home, at school, and in their community. Have each student write his name, in capital letters, vertically on the left side of a piece of notebook paper. Beside each letter of his name, instruct the child to record a heroic deed he can do that begins with that letter. While students complete their acrostic poems, have each student, in turn, come up to the front of the classroom. Using an overhead projector, create his silhouette by tracing the profile of the student's head onto bright-colored paper. Have each student carefully cut out his silhouette. After the student has revised and edited his poem, have him record it on his silhouette. Display these profiles and poems on a board with a black background. In bright letters add the title "Profiles Of Student Heroes."

Rover

Rover Saves The Day!

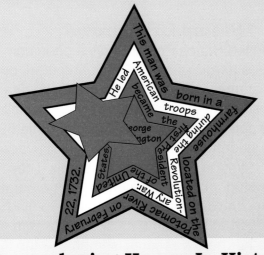

Remembering Heroes In History

Each year we celebrate Memorial Day to honor war heroes who have given their lives for our country. Encourage your students to honor all men and women—both living and dead—who have served during a war or conflict to protect our liberty and freedom. Assign each student one war hero to research (see list in box). Instruct each student to find information about his hero's birthdate and death date, the war(s) during which he or she served, any major accomplishments, and any awards or commendations. Duplicate the star patterns on page 62 for each student to use to create tracers. First instruct the student to cut out the pattern along the outside edges of the largest star. Have him trace this star onto red paper, cut out the red star, and set it aside. Then have the student cut the original pattern to the next star's edges, trace this star onto white paper, cut out the white star, and set it aside. Have the student continue this process until he has the following: one large red, one white, one blue, and two small red star cutouts.

Have each student glue the first four stars on top of one another (see the example shown above). Instruct the student to record a different clue about the identity of his hero around the edges of each star—beginning with the hardest clue on the large red star and ending with the easiest clue on the blue star. Direct the student to write the name of his hero only on the smallest red star in the center of his series. Then have him use tape and the remaining small red star to create a flap to hide the name of his hero. Mount these stars to create a colorful and interactive bulletin board for your room. Add the title "Heroes Worth Remembering."

War Heroes

War Of 1812: William Henry Harrison, Andrew Jackson
Civil War: Clara Barton, Ulysses S. Grant, Robert E. Lee
World War I: John J. Pershing, Eddie Rickenbacker
World War II: Henry H. Arnold; Omar N. Bradley; Dwight D. Eisenhower; William F. Halsey, Jr.; George C. Marshall; Chester W. Nimitz; George S. Patton, Jr.; Joseph W. Stilwell
Korean War: Douglas MacArthur, Matthew B. Ridgway
Vietnam: William C. Westmoreland
Persian Gulf: Colin L. Powell, H. Norman Schwarzkopf

Heroes Come In All Shapes And Sizes

Explore the concept of *heroes* further by reading aloud the book *The Hero Of Bremen* as retold by Margaret Hodges (Holiday House, Inc.; 1993). Discuss the main character—a crippled cobbler named Hans—and how he becomes a hero to his village. Discuss how Hans deals with the challenges of his physical limitations. Ask students to explain what Roland meant when he told Hans that "heroes come in all shapes and sizes. ..." Challenge students to offer support for Roland's statement by citing other individuals who have risen above physical limitations to perform heroic deeds that have benefited others.

55

A Hero's Legacy

Who are your students' personal heroes? Instruct each student to think of one person whom he looks to as a hero. The hero may be a famous person, a family member, or even a stranger who was there to help during a time of need. Have the student draft a list of words and phrases that describe the qualities and accomplishments of his hero. Then have the student use his list to create a poem, similar to a haiku, that commemorates this hero. Explain that the poem should contain 17 syllables divided into three lines of five, seven, and five syllables. Next direct the student to think of an item that represents his hero. For example, a *basketball* shape could represent *Michael Jordan*. Have the student create a colored cutout of this item. Then have the student record his poem once on each side of the cutout. Punch a hole in the top of the shape, and use fishing line and a paper clip to hang the hero poem from the ceiling of your classroom.

Stamp Of Approval

The United States Postal Service often commemorates heroic people by picturing them on postage stamps. Have students create original postage stamps featuring space heroes. Duplicate one copy of the stamp pattern on page 58 for each student. Assign each student a space explorer from the list below to research. Then have the student design a stamp commemorating the accomplishments of her hero. Remind the student that her stamp must visually communicate her hero's accomplishments to the public. Bind these stamps into an album titled "Space Heroes Who Have Earned Our Stamp Of Approval."

Edwin E. Aldrin, Jr.	Fred W. Haise, Jr.
Neil Armstrong	Mae C. Jemison
Guion S. Bluford, Jr.	James A. Lovell, Jr.
Roberta Bondar	Christa McAuliffe
M. Scott Carpenter	Sally K. Ride
Michael Collins	Walter M. Schirra, Jr.
Charles Conrad, Jr.	Harrison H. Schmitt
Leroy G. Cooper, Jr.	Alan B. Shepard, Jr.
Marc Garneau	Edward H. White, II
John H. Glenn, Jr.	John W. Young
Virgil I. Grissom	

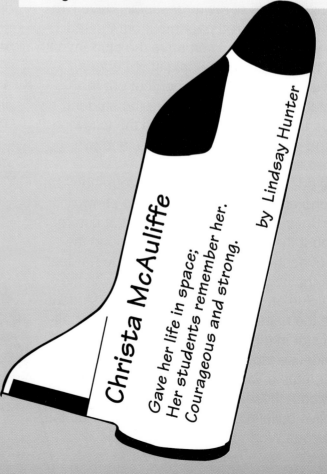

Christa McAuliffe

Gave her life in space;
Her students remember her.
Courageous and strong.

by Lindsay Hunter

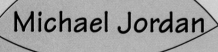

Michael Jordan

Calm, cool, collected;
Dribbles at the free throw line.
Great under pressure.

by Tommy Spann

Happy Birthday, Hero!

Here's a festive way to remember heroes throughout the year. Cut a class supply of paper strips. On each strip write the name of a school month. Fold each strip and place the strips in a jar. Invite each child to pull one strip from the jar. Have the student research a hero who was born during that month. Provide each student with a copy of the pattern below. Challenge her to use the information she gathered about her hero to design a birthday cake that reflects the characteristics and personality of her hero. For example, a birthday cake for hero *Paul Revere* could be decorated with *a lantern, a horse,* and *an American flag.* Gather and store the completed birthday cakes; then post the heroic birthday cakes for each month next to that month's calendar display.

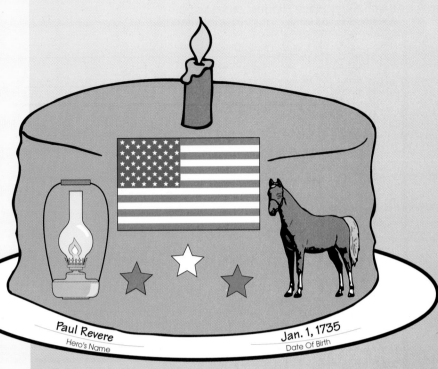

Paul Revere
Hero's Name

Jan. 1, 1735
Date Of Birth

Pattern
Use with "Happy Birthday, Hero!" above.

Hero's Name

Date Of Birth

Pattern

Use with "First-Place Heroes" on page 50.

1996 The Education Center, Inc. • *MAY* • TEC210

Pattern

Use with "Stamp Of Approval" on page 56.

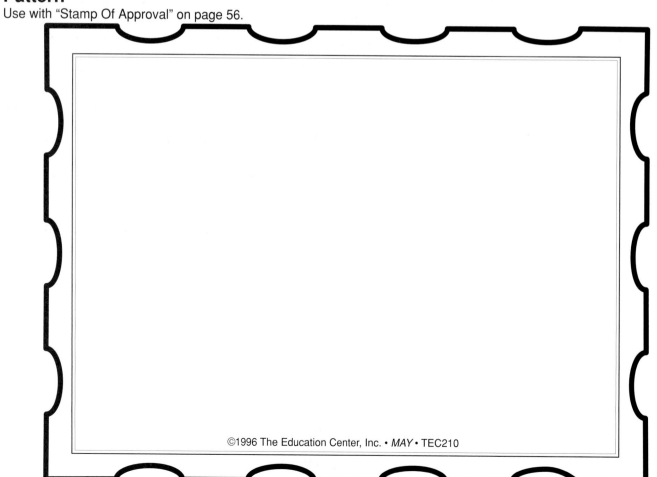

©1996 The Education Center, Inc. • *MAY* • TEC210

©1996 The Education Center, Inc. • *MAY* • TEC210

Names _____ *Critical thinking*

Only The Best Will Do!

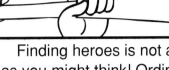

Finding heroes is not as difficult as you might think! Ordinary people do heroic things every day.

Directions: Work as a group to complete these activities.

A. What does it take to be a hero? Use the lines provided to list the characteristics of a hero.

1. _____
2. _____
3. _____
4. _____
5. _____
6. _____
7. _____
8. _____
9. _____
10. _____

B. Name five individuals who are heroes based on the characteristics your group listed.

1. _____
2. _____
3. _____
4. _____
5. _____

Note To The Teacher: Use with "Humming A Tune For A Hero" on page 51.

Pattern

Duplicate one copy of this page and page 61 for each student, and use them with "Hero Sandwich" on page 53. Also provide each student with glue, scissors, colored pencils, a black marker, one toothpick, two 1-inch pieces of clear tape, and poppy or sesame seeds. Provide a stapler.

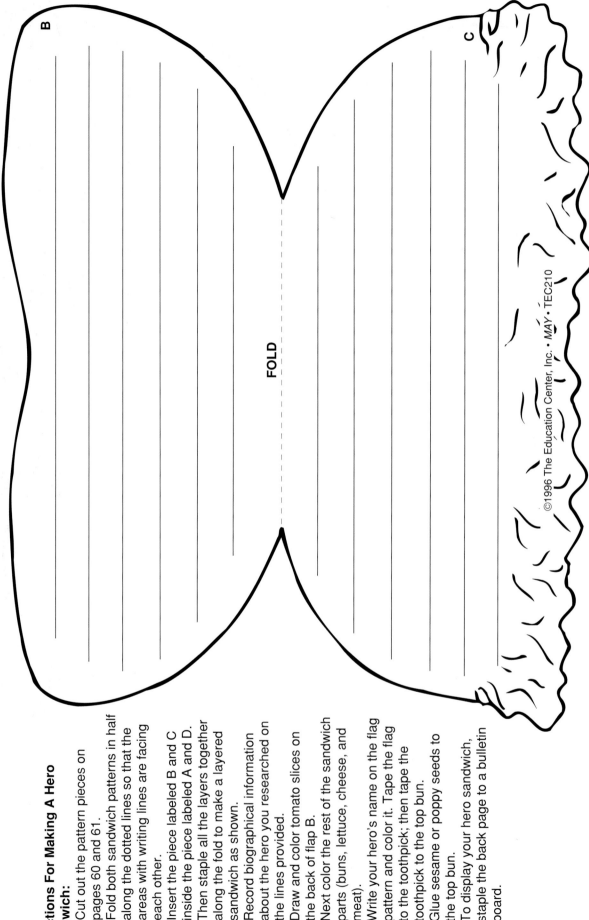

FOLD

B

C

Directions For Making A Hero Sandwich:

1. Cut out the pattern pieces on pages 60 and 61.

2. Fold both sandwich patterns in half along the dotted lines so that the areas with writing lines are facing each other.

3. Insert the piece labeled B and C inside the piece labeled A and D. Then staple all the layers together along the fold to make a layered sandwich as shown.

4. Record biographical information about the hero you researched on the lines provided.

5. Draw and color tomato slices on the back of flap B.

6. Next color the rest of the sandwich parts (buns, lettuce, cheese, and meat).

7. Write your hero's name on the flag pattern and color it. Tape the flag to the toothpick; then tape the toothpick to the top bun.

8. Glue sesame or poppy seeds to the top bun.

9. To display your hero sandwich, staple the back page to a bulletin board.

Patterns

Duplicate one copy of this page and page 60 for each student, and use them with "Hero Sandwich" on page 53.

A

D

FOLD

Completed Sandwich

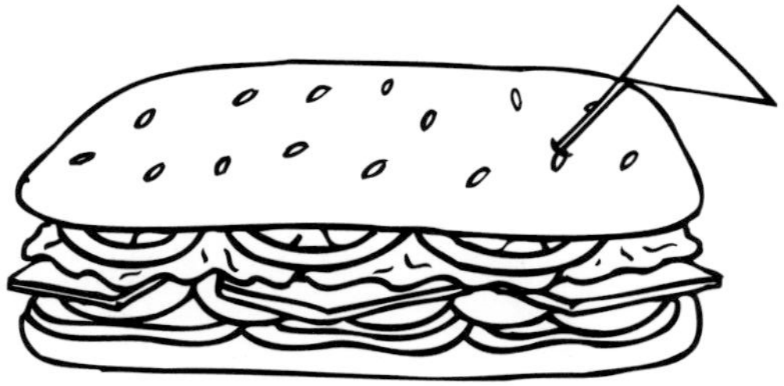

Flag Pattern
Cut out and record the name of the hero you researched on the flag.

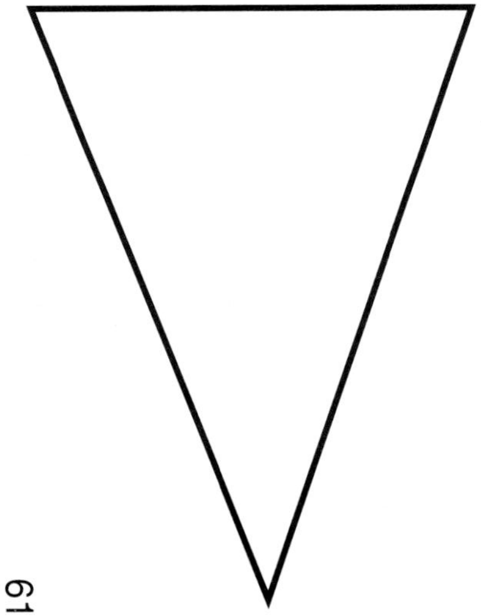

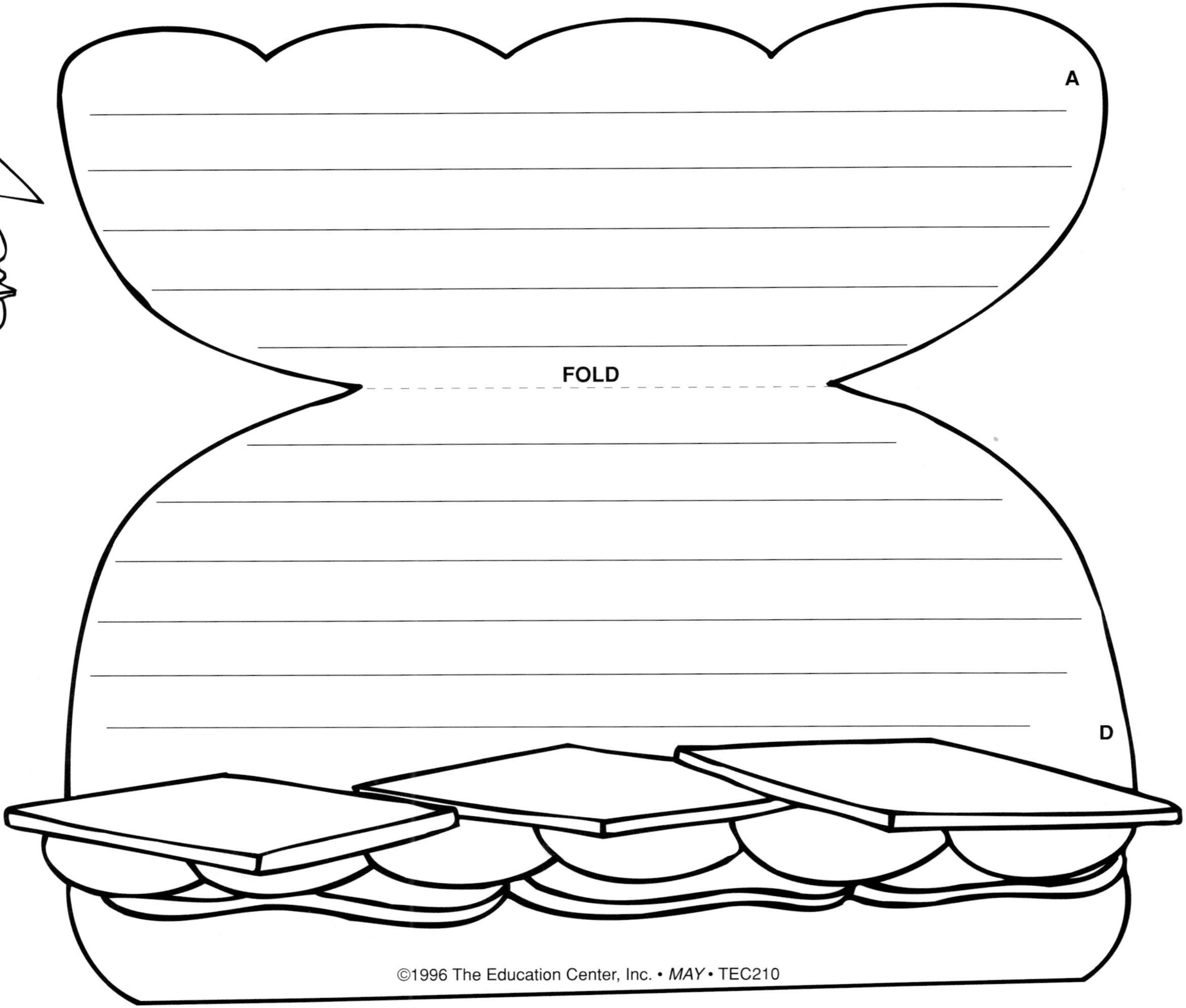

Pattern

Duplicate this page onto heavy paper for each student. Use the patterns with "Remembering Heroes In History" on page 55.

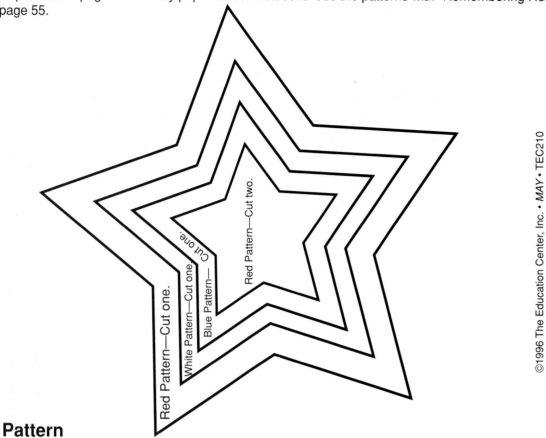

Red Pattern—Cut one.

White Pattern—Cut one

Blue Pattern— Cut one.

Red Pattern—Cut two.

Pattern

Use with "First-Place Heroes" on page 50 and "Hometown Heroes" on page 53.

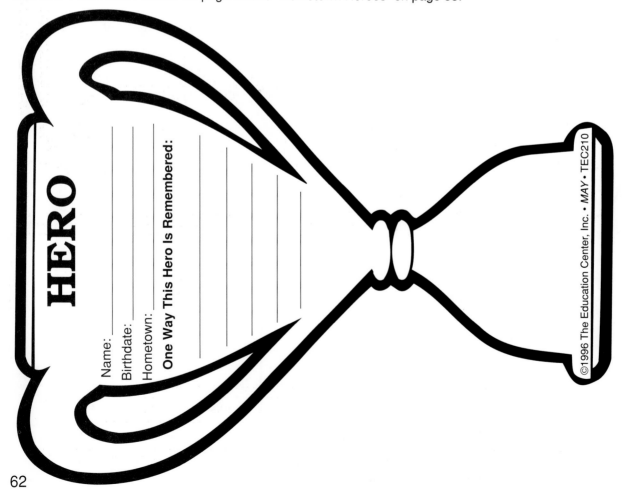

HERO

Name: _____

Birthdate: _____

Hometown: _____

One Way This Hero Is Remembered:

_____

_____

_____

_____

_____

Hooray For Heroes!

You've learned a lot about heroes in this unit. Now it's your turn to create a superhero of your own!

Directions: Use the space provided below to draw your superhero. Fill in the information to create your superhero's biography. Write your hero's name in the banner.

Superhero's Name _____

Height _____

Weight _____

Home _____

_____

Friends/Enemies _____

_____

_____

Physical Features _____

_____

_____

Unique Qualities _____

_____

_____

Special Abilities _____

_____

_____

Good Deeds _____

_____

_____

Other _____

_____

Comic Strip: Create a comic strip featuring your superhero in the spaces provided.

Bonus Box: Design a cover for a comic book featuring a story about the superhero you described above.

Note To The Teacher: Duplicate this page for each student. Provide each student with thin markers or crayons for coloring his or her superhero, the comic strip, and the cover.

Mastering Mysteries

Everyone loves a good mystery story. May 22 marks the birthday of the great mystery writer, Sir Arthur Conan Doyle. Use the following creative activities to help your students master mysteries. Even your students will be saying, "It's elementary!"

by Carol Felts and Dr. Linda Flynn

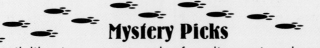

Mystery Picks

Pick from the following activities to weave a web of excitement and suspense for your mystery unit:

- Assemble a wide range of age-appropriate mystery books for your students to enjoy. Arrange the books in an old trunk or large briefcase.
- Set up an area of your room that is conducive to reading a mystery story. Bring in an old, overstuffed chair; a dim light; and a gently-ticking clock. Encourage your students to use the center to grab a few minutes of mystery reading during free time.
- Create a resource of mystery story ideas that students can later refer to for inspiration when writing original stories. Divide a three-ring binder into the following sections: traits of the sleuths, suspects, and witnesses; settings; clues; investigative techniques; and plotlines. As students come upon these characteristics in their reading, have them record details and ideas in the appropriate sections.
- Students love games, and what better mystery game to play than Clue®? Allow your children to play the game during recess or free time.
- Have each student create a "Top Secret" folder out of 12" x 24" paper. Instruct the student to use it to store important papers, work, or notes to parents.
- Direct each student to record on a piece of paper five things about himself that his classmates probably do not know. Collect the papers, and each day share the clues written by one of the students. Your class will have fun trying to guess the name of the "mystery student."
- Encourage students to watch the news or read the newspaper for local or national stories that are mysterious in nature. Use these stories to sharpen deductive reasoning skills. Discuss possible explanations for what actually happened and why or how events occurred. Also discuss possible suspects and witnesses.
- Read a mystery story aloud to your students. Afterward have your students create a puppet show based on the story. Arrange to have your class perform the puppet show for other classes during lunchtime. Call the production "Mystery Lunch Theater."

Classroom Crime Scene

How sharp are your students' sleuthing skills? One morning before students enter the classroom, remove something that they would notice is missing, such as a television, overhead projector, or computer keyboard. After the students are settled, act like you've just noticed that the item is missing and begin a search for it. Ask the students "How can we find the item?" (bring up the term *clues*), "Who was in the room last?" (discuss what a *witness* is), "Was anyone suspicious nearby?" (introduce the term *suspect*). Next tell them that in order to find the missing item, they will need to *investigate* what happened to it, just like a *detective* does. Retrieve the missing item. Explain that if the item were really missing, its whereabouts would be a *mystery*—which just happens to be the topic of the next unit of study.

Mapping Out A Mystery

What makes a mystery a mystery? Have students think about mystery stories they have read, heard, or seen on television. Ask them to identify what makes a mystery story different from other types of stories. Copy the semantic map above onto the board. Write the word *mystery* in the center circle; then, using the map as a guide, brainstorm characteristics of mysteries with the class. Give examples of each characteristic.

Next have each student choose his favorite mystery story. Instruct the student to complete a mystery map for his story (see the sample diagram). For instance, in *The Westing Game* by Ellen Raskin, Turtle Wexler (sleuth) tries to find out who in her apartment building murdered the millionaire Sam Westing (setting/crime/victim). Using clues, observation and deductive reasoning skills, and a lot of persistence (investigative techniques), Turtle determines who committed the crime.

Hang the completed maps on a wall or bulletin board titled "Mapping Out Mysteries."

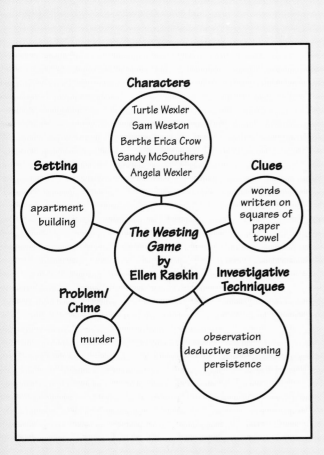

65

Cook Up A Good Mystery!

Help your students cook up their own mysteries using their classmates' zesty story recipes. Duplicate the recipe-card pattern on page 69 for each student. Direct the student to fill in the card with original mystery story elements including a title, the names and descriptions of characters (sleuth, suspects, witnesses), the crime scene (setting), the plotline, as well as any special directions to the writer. Then have the student cut out his recipe card. Make several photocopies of each student's recipe and place them in a folder. Draw and cut out a large pot as shown, and place it on a bulletin board. Arrange the original cards on the bulletin board around the pot. Then allow each student to go to the board, read the recipes, and choose one. Have him take a copy of his chosen recipe from the folder and use the ingredients to write an original mystery story. Display each student's completed mysterious creation next to its recipe card on the bulletin board.

Mystery Guest

It's no mystery that the best person to answer students' questions about mysteries is a detective. Invite a local police detective to speak to your students about the methods and tools he uses to investigate and solve a real-life mystery.

Add a mysterious spin to the visit by not telling your students that a guest is coming. On the day of the visit, have the detective come into the classroom unannounced for a few minutes, chat with you briefly, then leave. After the detective leaves, tell each student to write down as many details about the person as she can remember (gender, physical traits, clothing, etc.). Share and compare the responses; then invite the mystery guest back into the room. Discuss the importance of observation and attention to detail when trying to solve a mystery. Then introduce the detective and have him share the details of his job.

It's A Frame-Up!

Sharpen your students' attention to detail with the following whodunit activity. Point out that keen observation skills and reliable witnesses are vital to solving a mysterious crime. Use the description guide at right to discuss the details that a valuable witness would remember. Next divide students into groups of four. Duplicate "The Suspects" on page 70 for each group. Distribute a different suspect to each group member. Instruct group members to keep their suspects hidden from one another. Next copy and distribute "The Frame-Up" on page 70 and "The Lineup" on page 71 to each group member.

Direct each group member to first observe and then write a detailed description of his suspect on notepaper. Next have him take a turn at becoming a *witness* by reading his description to his group. As the description is read, direct the other group members to study their lineup patterns and listen for clues that will help them determine which suspect from the lineup is being described. Direct each group member to write the name of his chosen lineup suspect at the bottom of one of the frame patterns; then have him cut out and glue the chosen picture from page 71 onto the frame. (Tell him not to share his choice at this point.) After all four descriptions have been read and each group member has chosen four suspects, have each witness reveal his suspect so that the other group members can check their guesses.

JAILHOUSE JIM

FAST-FINGERS FRAN

Name _Matthew Bruck_

WANTED!

Name: _Dan Damson_
Otherwise known as: _Dead-Eye Dan_
Wanted for: _stealing chickens from a local farmer_
Height: _6 feet 2 inches_
Weight: _210 pounds_
Hair/Eye color: _red hair and green eyes_
Distinguishing features/marks: _wears a patch over his left eye (he lost his eye in a fight with a chicken), has a mole on the end of his nose, and has a scar on his chin_
Last seen wearing: _blue overalls, a red checkered shirt, a straw hat, and a blue bandana around his neck_
Last seen around: _Old MacDonald's Farm_

Wanted!

Follow up the above activity by giving students a chance to create their own suspicious characters. Explain to students that sometimes the faces and descriptions of criminals or suspects are placed on wanted posters in hopes that they will be recognized—and ultimately caught. Copy and distribute the wanted-poster pattern on page 69 for each student. Direct each student to create and draw a picture of a character who is wanted for a crime. Challenge the student to include as many descriptive details as possible (using the Witness Description Guide above for help). Then, on the back of the page, have the student write a story detailing events that lead to the capture of this criminal.

Junior Mystery Writers

Take the mystery out of writing mysteries by exploring *The Mysteries Of Harris Burdick* by Chris Van Allsburg. According to Van Allsburg's fictitious introduction, a man named Harris Burdick presented 14 intriguing illustrations and their matching captions to a publisher. Although Burdick promised to return with the accompanying stories, he never came back. The publisher published the pictures anyway.

After sharing the book with your students, have the class choose one of the 14 illustrations. Discuss the mystery behind the picture. Display the story map below and use it to guide your students in identifying and creating possible elements of the picture's story. Collaborate to complete a class story to accompany that picture.

Next have each student choose one of the remaining pictures. Have her use the web below to help her organize and write her own mystery story.

Check The Files!

Here's another option to help your students organize their Harris Burdick mystery stories. Copy and distribute the patterns on pages 72 and 73 for each student to use in organizing the elements of her story. Instruct the student to write one story element on each minipage pictured on page 72; then have her cut out each minipage. Next direct the student to cut along the dotted line of each file opening on page 73. On the back of page 73, have the student spread a thin line of glue under the bottom edge of each file folder. Then have her press the file-folder page to a blank sheet of 8 1/2" x 11" paper. Once the glue has dried, tell the student to arrange her minipages in the appropriately marked files. Direct the student to use her files to write a mystery story.

Use with "Cook Up A Good Mystery!" on page 66.

A Mystery Morsel From The Sleuthlike Mind Of:

____

(Your Name)

____

(Book Title)

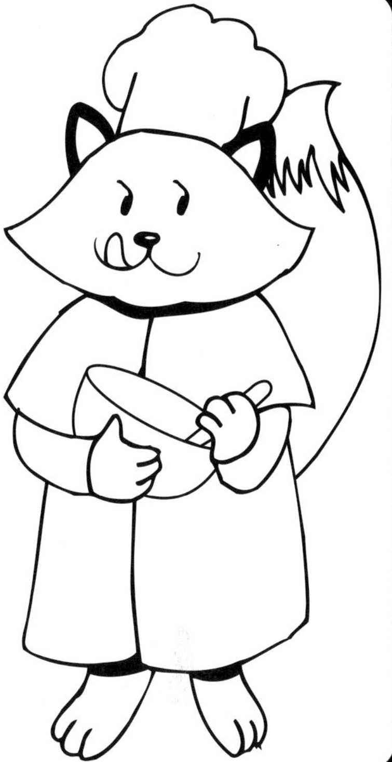

Ingredients:

______________________________ ______________________________

______________________________ ______________________________

______________________________ ______________________________

______________________________ ______________________________

______________________________ ______________________________

______________________________ ______________________________

Directions:

____

____

____

Use with "Wanted!" on page 67.

Name ______________________________

WANTED!

Name: ______________________________

Otherwise known as: ______________________________

Wanted for: ______________________________

Height: ______________________________

Weight: ______________________________

Hair/Eye color: ______________________________

Distinguishing features/marks: ______________________________

____

Last seen wearing: ______________________________

____

Last seen around: ______________________________

The Suspects

Irving

Mary

Molly

Oscar

Patterns Use with "It's A Frame-Up!" on page 67.

The Frame-Up

Name Of Suspect

Name Of Suspect

Name Of Suspect

Name Of Suspect

The Lineup

Louie

Albert

Matilda

Spanky

Oscar

Harry

Suzie

Bertha

Mary

Charlene

Gilbert

Benny

Molly

Sarah

Irving

Honey

Pattern Use with "Check The Files!" on page 68.

Name _____

A Master Of Mystery

Solution:
Describe how the mystery is solved.

Theme/Lesson:
Describe a lesson learned in the story.

Events:
Describe the events that lead up to the mystery.

Clues:
Describe the clues that are left behind.

Investigative Techniques:
Describe the techniques that the sleuth uses to solve the mystery.

Witness:
Describe his/her looks, words, and actions.

Suspect:
Describe his/her looks, words, and actions.

Problem/Mystery:
Describe the mystery that occurs.

Setting:
Describe when and where the story takes place.

Victim:
Describe his/her looks, words, and actions.

Sleuth:
Describe his/her looks, words, and actions.

©1996 The Education Center, Inc. • *MAY* • TEC210

Note To The Teacher: Use with "Check The Files!" on page 68. Give each student a copy of page 72, glue, scissors, and a blank sheet of paper. If desired, use this page as a guide to help students write additional mystery stories.

Bon Voyage!

Teacher-Tested Activities For The End Of The Year

Before your students pack up their bags—and their minds—for summer vacationland and camp, grab their attention with these motivating activities.

by Chris Christensen, Beth Gress, and Thad McLaurin

Been There; Done That!

What memories and experiences will your students take with them after this school year? Find out by having each student complete the following activity. Duplicate the suitcase pattern on page 81 for each student. Brainstorm several examples for each topic to get students thinking. Instruct each student to fill in the information on his suitcase, then color and cut it out. Enlarge, color, and laminate the traveler pattern on page 82. Mount all the suitcases and the traveler on a bulletin board as shown. If desired, add photographs of class events that took place throughout the year. Encourage each student to read his fellow classmates' reflections.

How Well Did You Do?

As a teacher, you've spent the year critiquing your students in order to improve their skills and increase their knowledge. Why not give your students the opportunity to help you polish your skills? This takes a "tough skin" and courage on your part; however, if you set the stage with a positive and serious attitude, you'll be pleased with the outcome. Duplicate page 83 for each student. Explain to your students that you value their honest opinions and prefer that each evaluation be completed anonymously. Assure students that you will analyze and use the results of the evaluations to help improve your program for the next year. Good luck!

On Top Of Old Smoky

There's nothing like a camp-in to keep your students motivated and well behaved until the end of the year! To conduct a camp-in, first set aside one to two hours on one day a week during the last month of school to pull the class together for some fun, camplike activities. Next make it clear that each of your students must earn the right to participate in each week's class camp-in by exhibiting good behavior during the previous week. Finally have students help you brainstorm the activities and events for each week's camp-in. Use the following list to get you started:

- Create a cool camp name, logo, and song.
- Plan a beans, chips, and franks lunch.
- Eat outside on picnic blankets.
- Turn off the lights and read a scary story by flashlight.
- Plan an art project suitable for a camp-in, like tie-dyeing T-shirts.
- Hold a class soccer, kickball, or softball game.
- Compete in a variety of relay races.
- Watch a video with a literature or curriculum tie-in.
- Have a popcorn party.
- Have a beach-theme party.
- Wear shorts, sunglasses, and straw hats; and play volleyball.
- Have a homemade ice-cream party.

After the list has been compiled, have students vote on the activities they would like to participate in on each camp-in day. Send a note home to parents explaining the weekly camp-ins and the behavioral requirements. Also request any needed supplies and volunteers to help with each week's camp-in activities. Make alternate arrangements for those students who do not earn each week's camp-in. Then start brushing up on your camp songs!

Let The Games Begin

Use a life-size version of tic-tac-toe to review concepts at the end of the school year. Give each student three 3" x 5" index cards. On the board list nine major subject areas your class has studied this year, such as Reading, Math, and Punctuation. Instruct each student to select three of the listed subject areas. On each of his cards, have the student write the name of the subject, a related review question, and its correct answer. Collect the cards and group them according to subjects. Add a few challenging, review question cards of your own.

Next create a large tic-tac-toe board on the floor with masking tape. Label each square with a different subject area. Divide your class into two teams: the X's and the O's. Instruct each student to write his name on a strip of paper. Gather the strips from each team in a separate container. To begin the game, draw a name from one of the containers. Direct the student whose name is drawn to select any square on the gameboard and stand on it. Then ask that student a review question from that subject. If the student answers correctly, he remains on the square. Then draw a name from the other team. When a student does not answer correctly, he must leave the square, and the other team gets to play. The first team to have three students standing in a row vertically, horizontally, or diagonally wins the game.

This summer I will ride my bike all over the neighborhood.

Science
Q. What is the chemical symbol for water?

A. H_2O

Spanish Science Health
Social Studies Writing Reading
Math Punctuation Spelling

Head Games

Enjoy a little summer fun with this crazy art activity. Have each student provide a head-shot photo of himself. Give each student a sheet of 9" x 12" white construction paper and one 3" x 5" index card. Instruct each student to cut out the head from his photo and glue it to the construction paper, leaving enough space underneath the photo to draw his body. Tell the student to draw his body enjoying a favorite summer activity, such as running, diving, or skateboarding. Once the student has completed drawing and coloring his body, direct him to cut out the completed figure. Then instruct each student to write a short sentence describing his favorite summer activity on the index card. Display the photos/drawings and their index-card captions on a bulletin board titled "Summer Fun, Here We Come!" Enlarge the sun pattern on page 84 and mount it in one of the upper corners of the board. Students will get a kick out of getting into each other's heads!

Have You Hugged Your Students Today?

Here's a special treat to let your students know how much you care. Duplicate a class supply of the "Have You Had A 'Hug' Today?" certificate on page 84. Complete a certificate for each student, including a compliment or a word of thanks or congratulations. Sign your name; then tape a Hershey's® Hugs™ candy to each certificate. Have other candy available for students who are allergic to chocolate. Pass out these certificates and watch your students enjoy a doubly sweet treat.

Social-Studies Box Games

Build on the enthusiasm that students have for games by having them work in pairs to create their own subject-review board games. Bring in a supply of board games for students to play in order to get familiar with a variety of layouts. Contact a local pizzeria to get a supply of donated pizza boxes (one for each pair of students). Divide your class into pairs and give each pair a pizza box; a resealable plastic bag; and art supplies for making playing cards, a spinner or a paper folded die, and game pieces. Then have each pair follow the directions below to conceptualize and design its game. After all the games have been completed, schedule a game day when the students can play each other's games as well as review their skills.

Student Pair Directions:
1. Select a subject-area topic you studied this year. Have the teacher approve your topic choice.
2. Design the layout of your gameboard on scrap paper.
3. Write a draft of your plan explaining the game's objective, strategy, and directions. Design your game so that players must use knowledge of the topic, as well as chance, to win.
4. Have the teacher approve your gameboard layout and the draft of your objective, strategy, and directions.
5. Transfer your layout design to the inside of the pizza box. Use as much space as possible. Decorate the remaining spaces with pictures related to your game's topic.
6. Research your topic and create playing cards for your game.
7. Write a final draft of your game's instructions.
8. Use the art materials to construct needed game pieces (a spinner, a die, etc.).
9. Write the name of your game and its authors on the outside top cover of the box. Also write the game's name across the front outside edge of the game box as shown.
10. Play your game to make sure that the directions are clear and correct. Make any necessary revisions.
11. Store any game pieces, playing cards, and the spinner or die in the resealable plastic bag. When the game is not in use, keep the bag of game pieces and directions inside the folded game box.

The Civil War Game

Math: graphing coordinates,
cardinal directions

SEARCHING FOR THE STAR

Directions:

1. Hide your star player on the grid by placing a star on a coordinate point. Label the point. For instance, (7, E). Do **NOT** show your grid to your opponent.

2. Take turns trying to locate your opponent's star player by guessing a coordinate pair.

3. Mark your incorrect guesses on your grid in one color so you do not guess them again. Mark your opponent's guesses in another color.

4. If your opponent guesses incorrectly, give him a directional clue using cardinal directions.

5. You score a **goal** and win the game when you find the exact coordinate location of your opponent's star player. Happy hunting!

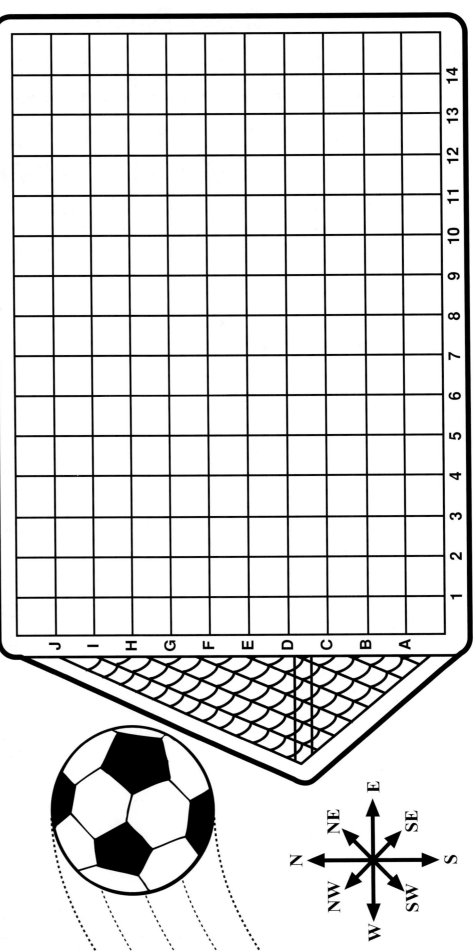

©1996 The Education Center, Inc. • *MAY* • TEC210

Note To The Teacher: Use with "Searching For The Star" on page 89.

DAFFY DECIMALS

Read each problem below. Decide if each number given makes sense in the problem. If it does, write "touchdown" in the space provided. If it does not make sense, move the decimal to correct the number. Then write the new number in the space provided.

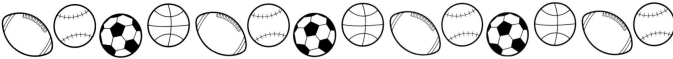

1. The Huskys' last volleyball game lasted 150.0 hours. _____

2. A Little League baseball team played a season schedule of 1.80 games. _____

3. During their last road trip, the Broncos covered 24.0 miles in four hours of driving. _____

4. Mike bought six new baseball bats for his team for $0.08. _____

5. Jeff Larmondra, heavyweight wrestling champion of the world, weighs 3.15 pounds. _____

6. In a basketball game, the winning team scored 7500.00 points and the losing team scored 73 points. _____   _____

7. Mrs. Smith's bowling ball weighs 80.0 pounds. _____

8. An average basketball hoop is positioned 0.10 feet from the ground. _____

9. Mr. Jones bought four hot dogs at a football game for $4.50. _____

10. Mike and Don played 180.0 holes of golf last weekend. _____

Read this article that's about to be printed in *The Sports Gazette*. Find the decimal errors and correct them so that the article makes sense before it goes to print.

In last night's championship game of the season, John Burnor, pride of the Patriot High School football team, scored an impressive 0.420 _____ points during his 40.0 _____ quarters of play. The junior, who weighs in at 1,822.0 _____ pounds and is 63.0 _____ feet tall, has spent his last 0.30 _____ years of high school helping his school win championships. John has been recruited by 1.1 _____ colleges. But after the exciting win last night, John told reporters that he's not sure he wants to leave his 0.05 _____ brothers and move away. We may be lucky enough to keep John right here in Monroe through the 1.998 _____ season.

Bonus Box: On the back of this page, write another nonsense decimal problem for a classmate to solve.

GOLF GOOF

You are the editor of *Sports In Review* magazine. Before leaving for his vacation, one of your writers, Dave Doolittle, dropped off an article for an upcoming issue. The article was supposed to list last year's top golf money winners in sequential order. When you begin to edit the article, you realize there are many mistakes. It looks like the corrections are up to you because the writer has left town. Order the prize winnings from greatest (#1) to least (#9) in the spaces provided.

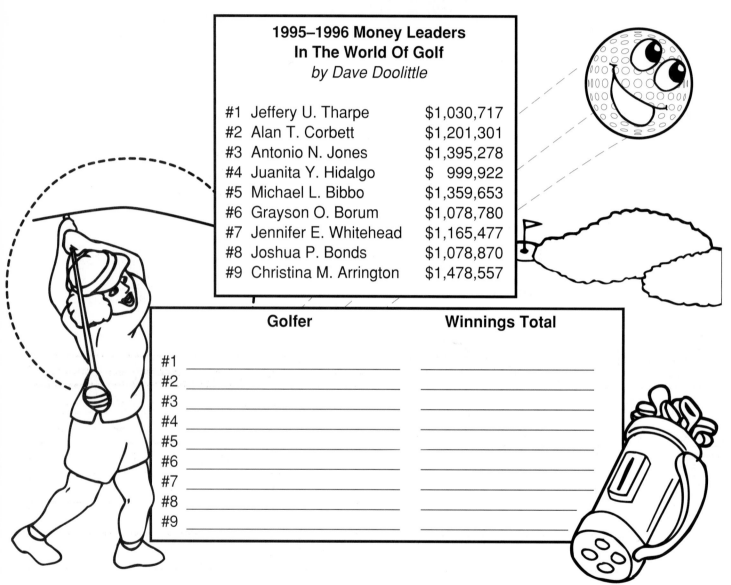

**1995–1996 Money Leaders
In The World Of Golf**
by Dave Doolittle

	Golfer	
#1	Jeffery U. Tharpe	$1,030,717
#2	Alan T. Corbett	$1,201,301
#3	Antonio N. Jones	$1,395,278
#4	Juanita Y. Hidalgo	$ 999,922
#5	Michael L. Bibbo	$1,359,653
#6	Grayson O. Borum	$1,078,780
#7	Jennifer E. Whitehead	$1,165,477
#8	Joshua P. Bonds	$1,078,870
#9	Christina M. Arrington	$1,478,557

Golfer   **Winnings Total**

#1 _____ _____
#2 _____ _____
#3 _____ _____
#4 _____ _____
#5 _____ _____
#6 _____ _____
#7 _____ _____
#8 _____ _____
#9 _____ _____

Using the revised version of the golf rankings, record the middle initial of the golfer in the blank that has the same number as his place in the rankings. If you have numbered the winners correctly, you will find out what Dave Doolittle has waiting for him when he gets back from his vacation.

___ ___ ___ ___ ___ ___ ___ ___ ___ ___ ___ ___!
#8   #2   #5   #1   #6   #3   #7   #9   #1   #5   #2   #4

Bonus Box: Calculate the difference in the winnings of the first- and ninth-place golfers.

©1996 The Education Center, Inc. • *MAY* • TEC210 • Key p. 96

Answer Keys

Page 29

1.
s
us
sun
Answers will vary.

2.
g
ag
mag
game
Answers will vary.

3.
m
am
may
mayo
Answers will vary.

4.
t
to
rot
toro
Answers will vary.

5.
o
to
cot
taco
Answers will vary.

6.
s
as
ask
mask
Answers will vary.

7.
a
an
pan
pain
Spain
Answers will vary.

8.
p
pi
pin
pain
paint
pinata
Answers will vary.

Page 45

Characteristics	Praying Mantis	Ladybug	Cockroach	Water Bug	Spider	Butterfly	Tick	Centipede	Bee	Chinch Bug
Three Body Parts (Head, Thorax, Abdomen)	✔	✔	✔	✔		✔			✔	✔
Six Jointed Legs	✔	✔	✔	✔		✔			✔	✔
Jointed Beak Or Straw For Sucking Liquids				✔	✔		✔			✔
Chewing Mouth Parts And/Or Sucking Tongue	✔	✔	✔			✔		✔	✔	
Leathery-Based Wings				✔						✔
I = Insect B = Bug O = Other Kind Of Arthropod	I	I	I	B	O	I	O	O	I	B

Page 46

1. Approximately 2/3
2. 10 years = 100,000
   100 years = 1,000,000
3. Answers will vary. No.
4. 88 degrees
5. 100 minutes (1 hour, 40 minutes)
6. 17,280,000
7. 10,950,000 eggs
8. 106,250 pounds

Page 49
Answers may vary.
Complete Metamorphosis
Stage 1: The egg hatches and a wormlike *larva* emerges.
Stage 2: The larva eats and eats, then forms a protective case around itself.
Stage 3: While in this case, the larva enters the *pupal* stage. The insect doesn't eat or move about during this stage. The larva slowly turns into an adult.
Stage 4: When the insect is fully grown, it splits open the pupa case and emerges as an adult insect.

Incomplete Metamorphosis
Stage 1: The insect begins as an egg.
Stage 2: The egg hatches into a small version of the adult insect called the *nymph.* The nymph looks somewhat like the adult insect, but is smaller and doesn't have wings and other adult features.
Stage 3: Finally the nymph molts and an adult emerges. The insect is now full-grown with all its adult features.

Page 93
1. 1.5
2. 18.0
3. 240.0
4. $80.00
5. 315.0
6. 75, touchdown
7. 8.0
8. 10.0
9. touchdown
10. 18.0

In last night's championship game of the season, John Burnor, pride of the Patriot High School football team, scored an impressive **42.0** points during his **4.0** quarters of play. The junior, who weighs in at **182.2** pounds and is **6.3** feet tall, has spent his last **3.0** years of high school helping his school win championships. John has been recruited by **11.0** colleges. But after the exciting win last night, John told reporters that he's not sure he wants to leave his **5.0** brothers and move away. We may be lucky enough to keep John right here in Monroe through the **1998** season.

Page 94
1. Christina M. Arrington $1,478,557
2. Antonio N. Jones $1,395,278
3. Michael L. Bibbo $1,359,653
4. Alan T. Corbett $1,201,301
5. Jennifer E. Whitehead $1,165,477
6. Joshua P. Bonds $1,078,870
7. Grayson O. Borum $1,078,780
8. Jeffrey U. Tharpe $1,030,717
9. Juanita Y. Hidalgo $999,922

UNEMPLOYMENT

Bonus Box: $478,635